D0961832

KIDS THESE DAYS

*Human Capital and
the Making of Millennials*

MALCOLM HARRIS
(B. 1988)

Little, Brown and Company
New York • Boston • London

Little, Brown and Company
Hachette Book Group
1290 Avenue of the Americas, New York, NY 10104
littlebrown.com

First Edition: November 2017

Little, Brown and Company is a division of Hachette Book Group, Inc. The Little, Brown name and logo are trademarks of Hachette Book Group, Inc.

The publisher is not responsible for websites (or their content) that are not owned by the publisher.

The Hachette Speakers Bureau provides a wide range of authors for speaking events. To find out more, go to hachettespeakersbureau.com or call (866) 376-6591.

ISBN 978-0-316-51086-8
LCCN 2017952769

10 9 8 7 6 5 4 3 2 1

LSC-C

Printed in the United States of America

For Lee, Tal, Ben, Annes, Steven, and Clark

Contents

Contents

KIDS
THESE
DAYS

Introduction

What is a generation? We talk as if they have breaks between them, like graham crackers or Hershey bars. But people don't couple and have children on a staggered schedule; there's a constant flow of newborns, with no natural divisions between Generations X, Y, and Z. What is it, then, that distinguishes someone born in one generation from someone born in the next? Is there a last baby on one side and a first on the other? Maybe it's like the Supreme Court on pornography: We know it when we see it. At its most basic level, a generation is when a quantitative change (birth year) comes to refer to a qualitative change. Over time a society mutates, and at a certain point in that development we draw a hazy line to mark a generation.

Since they aren't strictly defined, generations are characterized by crises, by breaks of one kind or another. Wars, revolutions, market crashes, shifts in the mode of production, transformations in social relations: These are the things generations are made of, even if we can only see their true shape in the rearview mirror. Every few decades American culture turns over, like a body rejuvenating its cells. But though reproduction is continual, the generations look at each other not over a line, but over a gap. The divisions are very real, even as they're also imaginary.

Because the way generations are defined is so hazy, it's easy to get away with less-than-rigorous analysis. If you say "the Selfie Generation," you're doing the work of defining and describing: The generation that takes selfies takes selfies. The few book-length considerations of Millennials—for our purposes I will mostly use this term to refer to Americans born between 1980 and 2000 (Reagan up to Bush II)—that exist are generally concerned with two things: young people's intellectual degradation, and how to manage them in the workplace. Shorter-form articles hem and haw about young Americans' romantic and sexual lives, our work ethic (or lack thereof), and especially our use of technology and the culture that has developed around it. Millennial stereotypes are just that, however, and stereotypes aren't a good place to start.

What these media accounts fail to present, even when their conclusions don't totally miss the mark, is a historical reason for what they're describing. To understand the consequences of a generational shift, we need more than just the proximate causes of new culture and behavior; we have to pull apart the tangled nest of historical trends where they hatched.

No one chooses the historical circumstances of their birth. If Millennials are different in one way or another, it's not because we're more (or less) evolved than our parents or grandparents; it's because they've changed the world in ways that have produced people like us. And we didn't happen by accident: Over the past forty years we have witnessed an accelerated and historically unprecedented pace of change as capitalism emerged as the single dominant mode of organizing society. It's a system based on speed, and the speed is always increasing. Capitalism changes lives for the same reason people breathe: It has to in order to survive. Lately, this system has started to hyperventilate: It's desperate to find anything that hasn't yet been reengineered to maximize profit, and then it makes those changes as quickly as possible. The rate of change is visibly unsustainable. The profiteers call this process "disruption," while commentators on the left generally call it "neoliberalism" or "late capitalism." Millennials know it better as "the world," or "America," or "Everything." And Everything sucks.

The growth of growth requires a different kind of person, one whose abilities, skills, emotions, and even sleep schedule are in sync with their role in the economy. We hear a sweetened version of this fact whenever politicians talk about preparing young people for the twenty-first-century labor market, and a slightly more sinister version from police officers and guidance counselors when they talk about working hard, flying right, and not making mistakes. It's tough love, and young Americans are getting it from all sides. This advice is uncontroversial on its face, but its implications are profound. In order to fully recognize the scope of these changes, we need to think about young people the way industry and the government already do: as investments, productive machinery, "human capital." If people have changed as much as other engines of productivity have over the past three or four decades, it's no wonder the generation gap is so significant.

By investigating the historical circumstances out of which Millennials have emerged, we can start to understand not only why we are the way we are, but in whose interests it is that we exist this way. In the wake of Occupy Wall Street, the mainstream media seems to have discovered increasing economic inequality, dramatized in the vastly unequal division of postcrisis "recovery" income. When it comes to age, this inequality manifests both between and within generations. Young households trail further behind in wealth than ever before, and while a small number of hotshot finance pros and app developers rake in big bucks (and big resentment), wages have stagnated and unemployment increased for the rest.

In the shadow of this high-stakes rat race, child-rearing has gone from harm prevention to risk elimination. It's no longer enough to graduate a kid from high school in one piece; if an American parent wants to give their child a chance at success, they can't take any chances. Entire industries have sprung up to prey on this anxiety, from Baby Einstein to test prep academies. For children born on the wrong side of the inequality gap, an increasingly integrated youth control complex puts them at constant risk of criminalization, from the classroom to the street to their bedrooms. The result is a generation of children with an unprecedented lack of unsupervised time who have been systematically denied the chance to build selves without adult oversight.

If this sounds like it might be anxiety-inducing, it should. Longitudinal studies on young Americans' psychological health reveal unprecedented changes. Young people feel—reasonably, accurately—less in control of their lives than ever before. Luckily, the silver lining of every twenty-first-century problem is a market niche, and youth psychosis is no exception. Long considered too indelicate a tool for developing minds, psychiatric medication has become part of a normal American childhood. Powerful pills can keep children who are at risk of malfunctioning under pressure operating on an ostensibly even keel. Depression and anxiety aren't just threats to our psychic and emotional wellbeing; when people's work depends on their communication skills and likability, mental illness is an error that must be corrected.

American kids spend more time on schoolwork than ever before, even though their skills with new technology make the performance of academic tasks like research and word processing much more efficient. A scholastic arms race has pitted adolescents against each other from a young age. For kids who have trouble competing—or ones whose fidgeting threatens the classroom discipline necessary for those who are—there are Adderall, Concerta, and other prescription uppers to keep them focused and productive. Of course, once the pills are on the playground, there's no keeping track of them, and the market sets prices for these study aids just like anything else. In a reversal of the traditional ideas about childhood, it's no longer a time to make mistakes; now it's when bad choices have the biggest impact.

If a Millennial does make it out of childhood on the "right track"—avoiding both the school-to-prison pipeline and debilitating psychosis (or even suicide)—and into higher education, there's no finish line. It's more like "Pass Go, Pay $30,000." The average college student takes out tens of thousands of dollars in loans from the government to go to school—tenacious debt it will likely take a decade or more to pay off, and on which default isn't a practical option. But with higher rates of enrollment, it's not enough just to attend college, especially given the costs; a degree has become a prerequisite, not a golden ticket. Meanwhile, the university has turned into a veritable industrial complex, complete with ever-expanding real estate holdings, hospitals, corporate partnerships, and sports teams that are professional in every sense of the word—except that the players work for free. And amateur athletes on whose talents a multibillion-dollar industry is built aren't the only ones asked to give their labor away: Unpaid internships have become the norm. Students are investing more time, energy, and money in their employability, and most of them have less to show for it. All of this raises the stakes for individuals; the worst off might very well be those in the category "some college," which means debt without the degree.

The whole school culture is built around hypercompetition, from first period, to extracurricular activities, to homework, to the video games kids play when they have a minute of downtime. It's not a coincidence—none of it. The growth of growth requires lots of different kinds of hard work, and Millennials are built for it. While cell phones and PDAs (remember when Personal Digital Assistants existed as a separate device?) used to be for businesspeople who billed for their time in minutes, now the average teenager has the tools to stay plugged in 24/7, and the training to use their gadgets better than those businesspeople can. Social media schools young people in communication and the emotional skills—as well as quick thinking and constant availability—that make them exceptionally productive. That also means they're populating these valuable new platforms with free content. When everyone is searchable and no privacy filter is reliable, kids learn quickly that everything they do goes on their permanent record—résumé and rap sheet alike. No one puts their whole self into their job like a Millennial who never learned to separate work and life enough to balance them, especially if they're wired on uppers and get anxious when they're too far away from their phone.

In the world of entertainment, media industries rely on the young artists whose cohort sets much of the country's cultural agenda. Near the close of the twentieth century, these media companies got extremely proficient at finding, identifying, and repackaging youth culture's rebellious side. "Selling out" was the scourge of Generation X, but a couple of decades later, the question is all but moot for young artists. The Faustian bargain with success is no longer about giving up your originality to be branded; now it's the artist's original brand the Man wants to buy. Whether trying to sell a rap album or a comedy series, young successes are expected to be successes already, with their own built-in fan bases, public brands, and professional-caliber media. With the spread of cheap recording, producing, and distribution tools, you no longer need to go to a label or a studio to make a market-ready album, music video, movie, or television show; you just need some friends who are practiced and willing to donate their skilled time. But to reap the rewards, you're going to need to beat almost everyone else just like you.

The business of sports has always fetishized young workers and is shifting with these advances as well. So-called amateur sports have grown (as an important part of the higher education industrial complex) and now constitute a multibillion-dollar market. Meanwhile, competition for the few scholarship slots and professional jobs for athletes has increased as teams look overseas to previously unexplored talent pools. Hyperrationalized training techniques and evaluation tools mean that promising child athletes are tracked and engineered from elementary school, which is also when they start learning about college scholarships. "Don't blow your ride!" is at least as old as *The Breakfast Club,* but with the price of higher education skyrocketing, the stakes are higher and the work is harder. For parents doing the tough math, turning an athletically or a musically gifted toddler into a prodigy might be cheaper than four years at a competitive private school. As long as the kid doesn't fuck it up.

Something is happening, whether we like it or not, whether we have a solution or not. A look at the evidence shows that the curve we're on is not the one we've been told about, the one that bends toward justice. We'd be foolish and naive to expect America's "moral universe" to progress independent of the other trends in our lives; it's nearly circular to say we are the people we become every day, but the progressive narrative doesn't allow for the flips and crises, the victories and defeats that make history such an eventful story. People match their circumstance, and vice versa; we're no exception. Without a recent historical accounting, we're stuck trying to understand young people based on a constellation of confusing behavioral data points. How are the same young people who were exposed to porn in childhood and are sending each other nude pictures by middle school also having less sex than their parents did? Why are we obsessed with the laziness and incompetence of the most productive workers of all time? And if college means better jobs, and more kids are going to college, why are wages down? Out of these contradictions the media has spun the story of the Millennial—a portrait that's right on some of the details, misguided on the rest, and totally wrong on *why*.

The moderate consensus view on American Millennials is that we don't represent anything new. Boomers and Gen Xers whining about us are creating moral panics out of the standard evolution of social and cultural habits, just like their parents did. It's true that the reaction to every successive set of tools and toys and their effects on our lives—especially the lives of children—sounds a lot like last year's and the year before's. Commentators worry about what cell phones do to our sociality, but before that it was Walkmen and long before that it was newspapers. And though it's fun juxtaposing covers of newsweeklies from different decades, all of them fretting about how this or that generation will be the end of us all, it also turns us into the boy who gets tired of crying wolf. But sometimes there is a wolf. It's worth an occasional check.

One of the consequences of "how we live now" is that we have more access to way more information about ourselves than ever before. This data is used to manage and control us in all sorts of ways—not the least of which is encouraging us to better *self*-manage and self-control—but it's also a tool in our critical hands if we choose to wield it so. A long hard look at the historical circumstances that have birthed Millennials can tell us more about our nature than any number of snapshot trend pieces or shallow surveys. The only way to understand who we are as a generation is to look at where we come from, and the social and economic conditions under which we've become ourselves. What I'm attempting in this book is an analysis of the major structures and institutions that have influenced the development of young Americans over the past thirty to forty years. That means parenting, schools, the criminal justice system, higher education, and the job market; it means looking at the changes in technology, psychology, sexuality, and other elements of social life that have shaped the adults Millennials are becoming. Without the full constellation, all we have is blinking epiphenomena: entertaining at a glance, but not enough context to guide a ship.

When politicians want to appeal to the public's better angels, they ask us to "Think of the children." Advertisers, civic agencies, parenting experts, psychiatrists, teachers, police: All of them tell us to ponder the effects our collective choices are having on the next generation. It's not a bad heuristic if you care about what's going to happen to your society, but the rhetoric is usually just used to sell one thing or another. Parents are treated like consumers, and "Think of the children" usually means "Think of *your* kid" and "Be afraid" and "Buy this or else." Maybe that's good advice for maximizing an individual kid's chance at success in a winner-take-all market, but we can see what kind of society—and person—results. When you look at some major trends in the lives of American young people, there's good evidence that the quantitative changes over the past three or four decades now constitute a meaningful qualitative rupture, one with repercussions we've yet to fully appreciate.

A hard look at these trends suggests that Millennials represent the demographic territory where a serious confrontation has already begun: a battle to see if America's tiny elite will maintain the social control they require to balance on their perch. It's not an arrangement they'll let go of without a fight, and they have a lot of guns—figurative and literal. Political reforms seem beside the point if the next generation's hearts and minds are already bought and sold. Millennials have been trained to hold sacred our individual right to compete, and any collective resilience strategy that doesn't take that into account is ill-conceived, no matter how long and glorious its history. A regular old political party with a social media presence is insufficient on its face. No one seems to know what *we*—with all our historical baggage—can do to change our future.

If, as blockbuster audiences seem to both fear and relish, America is quickly headed for full-fledged dystopia, it will have gone through us Millennials first, and we will have become the first generation of true American fascists. On the other hand, were someone to push the American oligarchy off its ledge, the shove seems likely to come from this side of the generation gap, and we will have become the first generation of successful American revolutionaries. The stakes really are that high: In the coming decades, more Americans will be forced to adapt in larger, stranger ways to an increasingly hostile environment. History asks different things of different generations; no child is born asking to go to war, and no number of shiny market-based distractions will make the next twenty years an enviable time to inherit America. But Millennials are going to be here regardless, and we have a lot of responsibility for whatever comes next.

Chapter One

Danny Dunn and the Homework Machine

Dear Kindergarten Parents and Guardians,

We hope this letter serves to help you better understand how the demands of the 21st century are changing schools and, more specifically, to clarify misperceptions about the Kindergarten show. It is most important to keep in mind that this issue is not unique to Elwood. Although the movement toward more rigorous learning standards has been in the national news for more than a decade, the changing face of education is beginning to feel unsettling for some people. What and how we teach is changing to meet the demands of a changing world.

The reason for eliminating the Kindergarten show is simple. We are responsible for preparing children for college and career with valuable lifelong skills and know that we can best do that by having them become strong readers, writers, coworkers, and problem solvers. Please do not fault us for making professional decisions that we know will never be able to please everyone. But know that we are making these decisions with the interests of all children in mind.

The above letter was sent to parents of kindergarteners at Harley Avenue Primary School in Elwood, New York, in April of 2014 to confirm rumors that the school would not be going ahead with its annual play.[1] The reason: These kids could not spare the two days off from their regularly scheduled work. *The changing face of education is beginning to feel unsettling for some people. What and how we teach is changing to meet the demands of a changing world.* Changes, changes, changes: It appears the kindergarten training of yesteryear isn't good enough. The implication is that the very *children* themselves aren't good enough without some serious improvement.

The "changes" are well known enough that the administrators at Harley Avenue felt comfortable using them to justify themselves without elaborating much. But what are these differences, exactly? Why and how are twenty-first-century American kids required to undergo more training than their predecessors? And what are the consequences for a generation raised on problem-solving to the exclusion of play? These questions are almost never at the center of popular discussions about contemporary childhood. Instead, authorities from the Brookings Institution[2] to *Time* magazine[3] to Matt Yglesias[4] have called for an end to summer vacation and the imposition of year-round compulsory schooling.

These drastic changes in the character of childhood are having and will continue to have a corresponding effect on society as the kids age. If America is going to reap what it sows, so far we seem only interested in *how much* we can count on producing, rather than what the hell it is we're growing. To adopt the scholastic euphemism "enrichment," America is trying to refine our kids to full capacity, trying to engineer a generation of hyperenriched "readers, writers, coworkers, and problem solvers." Parents, teachers, policymakers, and employers are all so worried that their children won't "meet the demands of a changing world" that they don't bother asking what kind of kids *can* meet those demands, and what historical problems they're really being equipped to solve. The anxious frenzy that surrounds the future has come to function as an excuse for the choices adults make for kids on the uncertain road there. As the Harley Avenue administrators put it, "We are making these decisions with the interests of all children in mind." How did we get to this place where we all agree that our kids need upgrading?

It behooves us then to begin with kids themselves, and the nature of American childhood around the turn of the twenty-first century. The work that kids do is going to play a major role in this book, and rather than start with, say, college students—whose workload is more obvious—and generalizing backward, I want to start with schoolkids, who are not generally considered workers at all. It's only by looking at children's work that we can understand the true reach of the changes in the past few decades.

1.1 The Pedagogical Mask

In America, unlike in much of the world, kids do not perform work. In this country, "child labor" evokes British industrialism, coal, and all things Dickensian. And though some American children have always worked—especially on farms—the dominant US view of childhood is as a time liberated from labor. Because children are legally excluded from the wage relation except under exceptional circumstances, children's work was reclassified as "learning." Jürgen Zinnecker, a sociologist of childhood, calls this process "pedagogical masking":

The working activities during childhood moratorium are disguised by pedagogical ideologies.... Learning is not understood as a type of work, whereby children contribute productively to the future social and economic development of the society. Only the adult work of teachers is emphasized as productive contribution to the development of human capital. The corresponding learning activities of pupils are thus defined, not as work but as a form of intellectual consumption.[5]

Removing the pedagogical mask is central to understanding the American economy because even if we don't see children's labor, the whole system rests on its unsteady foundation. It takes a lot of work to prepare yourself to compete for twenty-first-century employment, and adults are happy to remind kids of this when it comes to "putting your nose to the grindstone" or "staying on the right path." Kids are told, "Treat school like your job." But when it comes to the right to organize, the dignity of labor, or minimum wage laws, down come the pedagogical masks, and students go back to being students rather than workers. It's a precarious position: America can no more afford to recognize children's work than it can afford for them not to do it. Meanwhile, disregarded and unregulated, the intensity and duration of this work have accelerated out of control.

One story from the early days of modern children's work is extraordinarily prescient about the way pedagogical masking is now used to hide more and more labor. *Danny Dunn and the Homework Machine* is an enduring children's book from 1958 by Jay Williams and Raymond Abrashkin about a boy named Danny and his efforts to cheat on his homework. Danny is a whiz kid who lives with his mother, who keeps house for an absent-minded science professor, and Danny has a habit of dragging his friend Joe into half-baked schemes. The book opens with Danny, who has set up two pens linked by a board and attached to pulleys and a weight so that he can write his and Joe's math homework at the same time. He laments, "If only we could save even more time. You'd think six hours of school would be enough for them, without making us take school home. If only I could build some kind of a robot to do all our homework for us…"[6]

Danny and his friends use the professor's cutting-edge computer to do their homework quickly, leaving more time for baseball and their other fun hobbies—like measuring wind speeds with weather balloons. These kids aren't slackers; they just have better, more self-directed things to do with their time than homework. When a jealous kid (appropriately nicknamed Snitcher) rats out the crew, Danny has to explain to their teacher, Miss Arnold, what they've been doing. Rather than concede that he's been cheating, Danny argues that all workers use tools to do their work better and faster and that students should not be prevented from doing the same. Miss Arnold, stuck in a corner, reframes the situation under the pedagogical mask: "Danny, I must admit you've got a serious point. I won't force you to stop using the computer. But I'm asking you for your own good not to use it. Children learn through practice. You'll have to take my word for it that it would be better for you to do your homework the old-fashioned way."[7] But Danny is too smart for that, and he counters that if modern things are not to be trusted he probably shouldn't study atomic theory. It's a contradiction: Kids have to be taught how to use tools that will help them reduce their work-time, without it actually reducing their work-time.

Although it's just a children's book, *Danny Dunn and the Homework Machine* sets up one of the huge conflicts of the second half of the twentieth century: whether laborsaving technology would benefit workers or owners. Will the computer lead to the kids working less or working more? Danny's situation is different from ours because he gets his hands on the computer before the adults in his life do, and if he had used it like a good Millennial—keeping it to himself, freeing up his time to improve his résumé—he would have been on the fast track to Harvard. Instead, he's out to increase his playtime, which means liberating his friends as well. (It's no fun playing catch with yourself.) Miss Arnold has to find a way to contain Danny's discovery before this clunky proto-Wikipedia permanently ends homework. With the help of Danny's mother, Miss Arnold not only develops a plan—she develops *the* plan that would determine the character of American childhood a half century later: She increases Danny's workload.

There are two basic things you can do with technologies that make work faster: reduce work-time or intensify work. If a widget maker makes 100 widgets a day full-time, and a new machine allows the worker to make them twice as fast, they can either make 200 widgets a day or knock off at noon. It's not hard to see which way it has gone in America. Some of the same technologies that make traditional office workers efficient are even better for primary and secondary school students. Writing essays, doing research, communicating for a group project: There's almost no part of being a student that hasn't been made easier by technology. But computers don't do work for you, something Danny and his friends learn when Miss Arnold gives them additional homework assignments. The computer makes the work more efficient—it eliminates or reduces the extraneous tasks, like flipping through books or blotting out typos with Wite-Out—but what it leaves is still arduous. It's the irreducible mental work computers can't do. Instead of being liberated to play baseball, Danny and Co. are up late into the night programming. At the end of the semester,

Miss Arnold reveals that they have won special homework awards—light compensation for so many evenings lost. The Luddites who smashed laborsaving machines two centuries ago don't look so crazy now. The kids would have been better off if they had never learned to code.

The story of the homework machine not only gives us insight into the way schoolwork has followed the same intensification trend as other forms of labor, it also shows us how children's labor differs from waged work. The only compensation Danny gets for his extra effort and accomplishment is the nontransferable award from his teacher—one that costs only the price of a shiny sticker. On the micro level, this looks like one educator's clever effort to maintain the pedagogical mask and trick a student into learning more than he meant to. But in the half century that followed, computers got exponentially faster, cheaper, and more connected. In the intervening years, teachers, parents, and policymakers spread the intensification strategy far and wide. Stickers and other cheap rewards proliferated. Danny is no longer a lone precocious child. American kids now find themselves in his situation: overworked, underplayed, gold-starred, and tired, wondering where all their time went.

When it comes to primary and secondary schooling, American adults are able to hold a few conflicting stereotypes in their minds at the same time. On one hand, it's generally acknowledged that students are doing historically anomalous amounts of homework and that competition for desirable college slots is stiffer. On the other, these same kids are depicted as slackers who are unable to sustain focused attention, entitled brats who need to be congratulated for their every routine accomplishment, and devolved cretins who can't form a full sentence without lapsing into textspeak. But the best way to observe the character of Millennial childhood isn't to make guesses about how they spend their time, it's to actually check and see.

Social scientist Sandra L. Hofferth studies how American children pass their days, using twenty-four-hour diaries completed by kids and their parents between 1981 and 2003. When it comes to school, technological advances haven't freed up any time for American kids. Between 1981 and 1997, elementary schoolers between the ages of six and eight recorded a whopping 146 percent gain in time spent studying, and another 32 percent between 1997 and 2003, making it a threefold increase over the time surveyed, in addition to a 19 percent increase in time at school.[8, 9] Kids age nine to twelve, like Danny, have sustained near 30 percent growth in homework, while their class time has increased by 14 percent.

Because of all the changes in the way we do labor over the time in question, it's hard to describe how big this accumulation of schoolwork actually is. Whereas the labor of classically employed workers is measured in both total output and wages, we don't measure a student's educational product except in arbitrary and comparative ways, like grades, standardized tests, and school awards. Pedagogical masking disguises the work kids are doing every day and discourages researchers and policymakers from bothering to measure it at all. At the same time, we know labor productivity has increased markedly during the time in question, and we know kids are among the most avid users of popular productivity-enhancing tools. Besides all that, common sense says it's easier to do almost every element of schoolwork than it was a few decades ago. For all these reasons, I feel justified in saying American children's educational output has grown steeply over the past thirty years. But what does educational output even mean, and how might we try to measure it? When kids do work under the pedagogical mask, where does the product go?

1.2 Kid-Shaped Capital

Waged workers receive money to mark their expended effort-time—even though it only represents a fraction of their total output. The student equivalent is the grade: We say a student has "worked for" or "earned" her marks; the return of graded papers or report cards resembles the passing out of paychecks; etc. In theory, a grade in a class in a semester represents a student's work and skill exercised over time, but grades are comparative. Still, postsecondary grades have been rising nationwide, in a phenomenon that frustrated commentators have dubbed "grade inflation." But inflation is the wrong economic metaphor: Nongrade measures of educational output—like students taking Advanced Placement classes or tests, or kids applying to college—have trended upward, along with labor productivity in other sectors. It's a twisted system that aspires to train every student for "A" work, then calls it a crisis when the distribution shifts in that direction.

The idea that underlies contemporary schooling is that grades, eventually, turn into money, or if not money, into choice, or what social scientists sometimes call "better life outcomes." The pedagogical mask is incomplete, insofar as everyone involved in education—not least of all students—recognizes that the work they do (or don't do) has an impact on their future wellbeing. In waged work we have the concept of valorization, which is the process by which laborers produce value above and beyond their wages and increase the mass of invested capital. But if no one is profiting off kids' scholastic work—teachers definitely don't count—where does their product go? In the quoted passage above, Zinnecker makes reference to "the development of human capital" as the sink for students' hidden labor.[10] What this means in the simplest terms is what the kindergarten administrators said in the letter at the beginning of this chapter: When students are working, what they're working on is their own ability to work. Human capital's rough paper analog is the résumé: a summary of past training for future labor. At its most technical, human capital is the present value of a person's future earnings, or a person's imagined price at sale, if you could buy and sell free laborers—minus upkeep.

The "capital" part of "human capital" means that, when we use this term, we're thinking of people as tools in a larger production process. We can track increased competition on the labor market with indicators like wages (stagnant) and participation (decreased)—it's cheaper than it used to be to hire most workers, and extraordinarily hard to find the kind of well-paying and stable jobs that can provide the basis for a comfortable life. The arms race that results pits kids and their families against each other in an ever-escalating battle for a competitive edge, in which adults try to stuff kids full of work now in the hope that it might serve as a life jacket when they're older. If they track into the right classes, and do their homework, and study, and succeed in the right extracurriculars, and stay out of trouble, and score well on standardized tests, and if they keep doing all that from age five to age eighteen, they'll have a good chance at a spot in a decent college, which is, as far as you can plan such things, a prerequisite to "better life outcomes." Of course, the more kids who can do all that, the harder everyone has to work to stay on top.

When it comes to the primary and secondary education pool, the "high-achieving" end has become a lot more crowded. Between the 1984–85 and 2011–12 school years, there was an increase of 921 percent in the number of high school students taking Advanced Placement courses, as well as an increase in the number of tests per student, from 1.37 to 1.76.[11] While you might expect that such an expansion would have a negative effect on scores, the percentage of students scoring the top marks of 4 or 5 on their tests stayed constant.[12] A passing score on a high school AP exam counts for credit at over four thousand institutions of higher education, and many of the schools that don't count them for credit still de facto require them for admission. They are supposed to have the rigor of college classes. The rate of AP class expansion is both example and index of the larger trend: A lot more kids are working a lot harder.

For a more micro example, see what happens when a grown man tries to do his high-achieving thirteen-year-old daughter's homework. For his 2013 *Atlantic* article "My Daughter's Homework Is Killing Me," Karl Taro Greenfeld attempted to complete his eighth grader's homework from her selective New York public school in an effort to discover the exact nature of the labor that was keeping her awake every night. He quickly discovered that he wasn't prepared to keep up: "Imagine if after putting in a full day at the office—and school is pretty much what our children do for a job—you had to come home and do another four or so hours of office work.... If your job required that kind of work after work, how long would you last?"[13] By Thursday, Greenfeld was using Google Translate in classic homework machine fashion (and in clear contravention of the rules) to complete a Spanish assignment. Of course, he tinkered with the results a little to avoid overt plagiarism. When he asked his daughter's teachers why they assigned so much homework, they either rejected responsibility or cited the importance of time-management skills.

This shift and its justification were foreshadowed once again by *Danny Dunn and the Homework Machine:* When the class groans about how much homework they're given, Miss Arnold answers, "You all know that the class has grown a good deal in the last couple of years. That means I can't work with each one of you as much as I used to. It means high school will be overcrowded, too. It also means that there will be more competition for college admissions. It's not easy to get into college these days."[14] The fact that there are more of them doing more work doesn't reduce the collective burden the way division of labor does in a group project. Rather, it *increases* the work each of them must do to keep up with each other and avoid being left behind. *Danny Dunn* was published over fifty years ago, in 1958, and things have gotten worse.

This sort of intensive training isn't just for the children of intellectuals; the theory behind the rhetoric advocating universal college attendance is that any and all kids should aspire to this level of work. College admissions have become the focus not only of secondary schooling but of contemporary American childhood writ large. The sad truth, however, is that college admission is designed to separate young adults from each other, not to validate hard work. A jump in the number of students with Harvard-caliber skills doesn't have a corresponding effect on the size of the school's freshman class. Instead, it allows universities to become even more selective and to raise prices, to populate their schools with rich kids and geniuses on scholarships. This is the central problem with an education system designed to create the most human capital possible: An en masse increase in ability within a competitive system doesn't advantage all individuals. Instead, more competition weakens each individual's bargaining position within the larger structure. The White House's own 2014 report on increasing college opportunity for low-income students noted, "Colleges have grown more competitive, restricting access. While the number of applicants to four-year colleges and universities has doubled since the early 1970s, available slots have changed little."[15] Still, the Obama administration remained undaunted and continued to champion universal college enrollment, as if we even had the facilities to handle that.

Human capital, from its midcentury retheorization by a group of economists at the University of Chicago, has always been about investment. If you're a manager who only sees employees as wage earners—they lend you their labor, you pay them for it afterward—you're ignoring a whole other set of relations. The logic of human capital, on the other hand, splits decision, action, and result into three aspects of the same person so as to quantify and scientifically manage life outcomes. First a kid decides to invest her time in math homework; then she spends the hours running through equations; the next morning she wakes up a more valuable future employee. Her investment at thirteen will bear fruit when, at her job years later, she'll be able to work herself more productively, generating more value for her employer than if she had spent that night in eighth grade getting stoned in her room listening to glitchstep and texting with her friends instead of doing math.

It's an elegant accounting, and one that can depict the real economic value of children's schoolwork. It also accords with our national rhetoric about effort, and about childhood as the time to accumulate the skills and abilities necessary to compete in a tough adult job market. The logic of human capital is now the basis for the American education system, which means it's the code that governs the day-to-day lives of America's children. This regime of universal measurement lends new meaning to the generic life advice we give kids about being their best and reaching their potential. In a world where every choice is an investment, growing up becomes a very complex exercise in risk management. The next question is how exactly society divides those risks—and the profits. Over time, firms have an incentive, as economist Gary Becker (a member of the University of Chicago group) put it in his landmark 1975 study "Human Capital: A Theoretical and Empirical Analysis, with Special Reference to Education," to "shift training costs to trainees."[16] If an employer pays to train workers, what's to stop another company from luring them away once they're skilled? The second firm could offer a signing bonus that costs them less than the training and still make out like bandits. Paying to train a worker is risky, and risk costs money. The more capital new employees already have built in when they enter the labor market, the less risky for their employer, whoever that ends up being. As American capitalism advanced, the training burden fell to the state, and then to families and kids themselves.

1.3 Risky Child-Rearing

Widening inequality means that the consequences of being caught on the wrong side of the social divide are larger, and parents are understandably anxious about their children's future prospects. Policymakers, employers, and teachers—not to mention various salespeople working their own angles—have parents convinced that the proper way to manifest care and affection for their progeny is to treat them like precious appreciating assets. Under these conditions, every child is a capital project. Rationalization—the tendency for firms to reduce every interaction to a number so that they'll be easier to optimize—has come to apply more and more to people themselves as productive tools. Risk management used to be a business practice; now it's our dominant child-rearing strategy.

In her study *The Playdate: Parents, Children, and the New Expectations of Play,* sociologist Tamara R. Mose details how parents of young children in New York City have turned child's play into anything but. The image of kids running around the streets of New York playing stickball and whatnot is ingrained in our national subconscious as perhaps *the* image of happy, independent childhood. But in a trend elapsing over the past twenty to thirty years, Mose sees parents holding their children in the home, exposing them only to screened peers, vetted activities, and even approved snacks. As a social phenomenon, playdates are something like private schools. Wealthier parents remove their kids from public and sequester them somewhere with a guest list and a cover charge. Mose uses the term "enclosure"—which is when a public or common resource is fenced and privatized. The territory of kids' play used to be a commons, and now it's been divided up into tiny, guarded pieces.

Playdates are also part of adult professional networking. Even children's birthday parties are a competition:

> The birthday party becomes a display of economic advantage and thus class advantage. By holding elaborate festivities for young children, parents are able to demonstrate their affluence, their sense of quality and quantity, their class worth. If a mother can put on an event that is considered "playground-worthy," her children will be considered worthy of holding playdates with, or their parents considered worthy of getting to know better. This angst creates a competition among groups of parents, thereby producing even more elaborate birthday parties.[17]

According to Mose, the biggest difference between simple play and an official playdate is that playdates are work. Playdates aren't just scheduled, they're prepared. They have expenses, and they can succeed or fail. A parent who serves the wrong kind of savory snack could be jeopardizing their family's place in the social hierarchy. Kids play, adults—or, more accurately, moms—make playdates. And not just any moms; playdates are an upper-middle-class practice, but it's that group that sets the national standards. As we'll see in the rest of this chapter, Millennial childhood norms weren't crafted for average or "normal" families. Now, up and down the class ladder, hands-off parenting is likely to attract glares and possibly even the attention of authorities. What kind of parent would risk their child's safety like that?

Playing in public isn't actually dangerous, at least not compared to the golden days. Death by unintentional injury for children under fifteen has fallen by more than half since the early 1970s.[18] The distinctions between good and bad playdate foods are, in Mose's analysis, mostly about branding. Whether or not something is organic is more important than its nutritional value. The real value is elsewhere, in the allusion to a certain kind of "good" parenting that lets others know that you're the right type of family, what Mose calls "People Like Us." Companies can charge for that.

Millennials grew up during this norm change, and it has shaped us as individuals and as a cohort. Children develop understandings of dynamics that they can't describe, and the idea that they don't know when they're being used to further their parents' professional networks (for example) is naive. All the class baggage around playdates sinks through their malleable skulls and into their growing brains. A cohort of kids has absorbed all the ambient nervousness around safety, even though it has never been particularly well founded in real danger.

"Safety" is a broad, nebulous concept, even as it's anxiously central to child-rearing. And kids could always be safer. "The ultimate question then becomes," Mose writes, "how do parents choose 'safe' people with whom to hold a playdate? 'Safe' in this context really means people/parents who are selected based on potential social and cultural capital."[19] The true risk of nonorganic food isn't that it's going to poison anyone, it's that the kids whose parents are buying it might not make for the best professional connections down the line, which means if your child plays with them, your child is less likely to get a crucial future promotion than they would be if they had played with peers who ate fancier corn puffs. This may or may not be an accurate analysis, but it must be confusing for young kids at first. That is, until they absorb the attention to class hierarchy. Childhood risk is less and less about death, illness, or grievous bodily harm, and more and more about future prospects for success.

To gain insight into the contemporary idea of childhood risk, British researcher Tim Gill focused on the changing composition of playgrounds. In his survey (although Gill focused on the UK, his research suggests that "risk aversion appears to be even more acute in the USA"[20]), he found that unwarranted fears about safety have led adults to cushion and overstructure their children's relations with the physical and social world. As he puts it in a disturbing and concise summary:

> Activities and experiences that previous generations of children enjoyed without a second thought have been relabeled as troubling or dangerous, while the adults who still permit them are branded as irresponsible. At the extreme...society appears to have become unable to cope with any adverse outcomes whatsoever, no matter how trivial or improbable. While such episodes may be rare, they fit a pattern of growing adult intervention to minimize risk at the expense of childhood experience.[21]

Over the final quarter of the twentieth century, parental time spent on child care increased dramatically for both women and men, single and married, across three different modes of measurement.[22] Combined with the growing time kids spend on academics and extracurricular activities, as well as time producing and consuming digital media, they are more watched than ever. This leads Gill to conclude, against the stereotypes of youth run amok, "Their lives are marked not by chaos and moral vacuum, but by structure, supervision, and control."[23]

Gill found that a fog of fear has enveloped the playground, from the exacting safety codes that have replaced wood chips with ouchie-proof rubber floors, to totally unjustified propaganda about interacting with strangers and an overreliance on "bullying" rhetoric to reduce the complexity of childhood conflict. The generalization of these fears "reinforces a norm of parenting that equates being a good parent with being a controlling parent, and that sees the granting of independence as a sign of indifference if not outright neglect, even though the benefits of giving children a degree of freedom to play, especially outside, are increasingly well documented."[24]

Researchers whose overriding concern is the welfare of children see this trend as unwelcome and even dangerous. In an article for the *American Journal of Play* on the decline in American children's free time, Peter Gray described what kids miss out on developmentally when they aren't allowed the space to self-direct:

> Even casual observations of children playing outdoors confirm that these youngsters, like other young mammals, deliberately put themselves into moderately fear-inducing conditions in play. Their swinging, sliding, and twirling on playground equipment; their climbing on monkey bars or trees; their risky skateboarding down banisters—all such activities are fun to the degree that they are moderately frightening. If too little fear is induced, the activity is boring; if too much is induced, it becomes no longer play but terror. Nobody but the child himself or herself

knows the right dose, which is why all such play must be self-directed and self-controlled. Beyond the physically challenging situations, children also put themselves into socially challenging situations in their social play. All varieties of social play can generate conflict as well as cooperation; and to keep playing, children must learn to control the emotions, especially anger and fear, that such conflict can induce.[25]

There probably aren't many parents, teachers, or even politicians who consciously decide they want to raise bored children and young adults who have trouble controlling their emotions. Yet these are the consequences of their actions. The problem is that risk management usually applies—as far as the managers are concerned—to piles of money, not people. Rationalization is called just that because, since everything is boiled down to the qualitatively equivalent dollar, there are no sentimental concerns to impede fully rational decision-making. There's no way to eliminate risk altogether, and assessing it rationally always means accepting a certain amount—ideally the exact right amount. But for a loving parent, a parent who has been told over and over that they should be willing to die for their children, what's the right amount of risk to accept when it comes to their son's or daughter's future wellbeing?

It is worth noting that the average American parent likely has fewer backup children than at any time in the nation's history. Family size shrank rapidly between the mid-1960s and the 1990s, so much so that by 2001 average family size (3.14) was where average *household* size (which included single people and couples) was in 1970.[26] Between 1976 and 2014, the number of women in their early forties with four or more children nose-dived, from over a third down to 12 percent.[27] This is in accord with Americans' wishes: Before the 1970s, the plurality of surveyed Americans said the ideal family had four or more children, but ever since, the dominant answer has been two kids. But even if that is what parents want, a perhaps unanticipated consequence has been more parental attention (and investment) concentrated on fewer children.

If it is every parent's task to raise at least one successful American by America's own standards, then the system is rigged so that most of them will fail. The ranks of the American elite not only aren't infinitely expandable, they're shrinking. Given that reality, parents are told—and then communicate to their children—that their choices, actions, and accomplishments have lasting consequences, and the consequences grow by the year. The letter at the beginning of this chapter is merely one of the more dramatic and unintentionally public examples of this fearmongering. Risk management combined with parental love has turned to *risk elimination*.

1.4 Helicopter Parents, Vigilante Moms, and Zero Tolerance

Childhood risk elimination takes two complementary forms: helicopter parents and zero-tolerance policies. The helicopter parent is the archetypically protective upper-class mom—sometimes dad—who takes direct personal responsibility for her child's schedule and time. Helicopter parents always know where their child is, what they're doing, and how whatever it is they're doing will help them get into college—always a good one, and sometimes even a particular college chosen in advance. In their study for *UC Davis Law Review* on overparenting, Gaia Bernstein and Zvi Triger tracked the growth in what they call "intensive parenting." The authors break the practice into three stages:

> First, parents acquire sophisticated knowledge of what experts consider proper child development in order to recognize and respond to every stage of the child's emotional and intellectual development. Second, parents engage in "Concerted Cultivation": parents actively foster and assess the child's talents, orchestrate multiple child leisure activities, and regularly intervene in institutional settings on the child's behalf. Third, to fulfill the same goals, parents closely monitor many aspects of the child's life.[28]

Bernstein and Triger track intensive parenting through its beginning at conception, to hand sanitizer for toddlers, an overabundance of field trip chaperones, and the emergence of school-to-parent digital telecommunications technologies. In both informal codes of conduct and formal statutes of law, intensive parenting has become the American standard. As the authors write after reviewing the relevant literature, "Many parents are increasingly incorporating defensive practices into their child rearing routines, often over-estimating risks and over-protecting their children."[29]

The intensive parent attempts total control for the same reason we don't have wooden playgrounds anymore: so nothing bad happens. Bad things that could happen include but are not limited to: the child getting hurt outside, the child being kidnapped, the child being placed in a lower academic lane, the child contracting a chronic illness, the child developing a drug addiction, the child using drugs, the child getting a bad grade, the child getting pregnant or getting someone else pregnant, the child having sex and contracting an STI, the child getting in a fight, the child being disciplined by the school, the child being disciplined by the police, the child being killed by the police, the child dropping out of school, the child not getting into a good college, and the child not getting into college at all. These are hazards any parent might worry about, but they're also things any *investor* might worry about. The easy slippage between these roles makes intensive parents ideal managers for budding capital, whether they think of it that way or not.

Mothers in particular tend to be responsible for the care of children in the first and last instances. When we consider all the work mothers do to keep children ready to succeed at school, it's clear their work gets hidden under the pedagogical mask as well; the education system could never survive a mom strike, and without the education system, American industry would be lost. When an individual child happens to be slow or just falls behind, it's usually up to the mother to make sure the child gets back on track and stays there. Teachers and guidance counselors can only provide so much individual attention, and navigating the school bureaucracy can be a full-time parent's job, depending on the child and the family.

In families with "problem children," mothers are trapped in one hell of a bind. For her study *Family Trouble: Middle-Class Parents, Children's Problems, and the Disruption of Everyday Life,* sociologist Ara Francis spoke with mothers of children whose "issues"—like autism, depression, or drug addiction—put them at the margin of mainstream success. She found that first these moms had to deal with self-blame and disappointment. (According to Francis's research, dads mostly get a pass from society as long as they're somewhat involved in their children's lives, which, to their credit, more and more fathers are.) In a culture that increasingly rewards only exceptional accomplishment, any disadvantage or challenge can seem like a disqualification. One mom told Francis that because she had expected her son to star on the football team, his ADD diagnosis made her feel the way a parent who had expected a "normal" child must feel upon hearing a diagnosis of Down syndrome.[30] It's an insensitive comparison, but there's something revealing in the equation: A hypercompetitive environment sets parents up for dreams of champion children, and then for almost inevitable heartbreak. Millennials of all abilities have grown up in the shadow of these expectations, expectations that by definition only a very few of us can fulfill.

In Francis's study, mothers blame themselves, but they also get some help. Parents, teachers, counselors, and other community members find moms culpable for their children's deficiencies by default, and the higher the level of competition, the more restrictive the mold, the higher the population of kids who don't measure up or fit in. Moms have to work harder to give their kids whatever boost they need to win—or at the very least finish the race—or else they're stigmatized. In her study *Raising Generation Rx: Mothering Kids with Invisible Disabilities in an Age of Inequality,* sociologist Linda M. Blum calls these moms "vigilantes" because, although they're not usually committing crimes, "a mother's unyielding watchfulness and advocacy for her child took on the imperative of a lone moral quest."[31] These vigilante moms are taking the law (or, rather, the school administrative bureaucracy) into their own hands, but it can't last forever. Francis writes that the only thing that reduces this kind of maternal stigma once and for all is aging: "It was particularly common for attention deficit disorder to be reframed in terms of character flaws, such as 'laziness,' as children grew older."[32]

There's a stereotype that these vigilante moms are all rich, and it's easy to confuse them with helicopter moms. There is overlap between the categories, which yields some understandable resentment: Do their kids really need *more* advantages? Do these moms really need to help further rig an already unfair contest? But that's not what Blum and Francis found in their research; they talked to many working-class mothers who were totally invested in giving struggling children their best shot, even if that just meant keeping them in a mainstream high school program. Being a vigilante is of course easier for moms of means, but they're a minority. The stereotype further buries the uncompensated labor of those working-class mothers who add full-time child advocacy to their list of jobs. Blum points out that single mothers find a special lack of support and extra judgment in a culture that still treats two-parent families as normal. All types engage in maternal bureaucratic vigilantism, but what happens to kids who don't luck into having Erin Brockovich for a mom?

Even mothers can't be there 24/7, and a rational society needs backup institutions and personnel. After all, some parents don't behave properly. Educational institutions have traditionally served in loco parentis, and their disciplinary philosophy has changed a lot over the past couple of decades. In the 1990s, "zero tolerance" policies swept the nation's schools. The American Psychological Association's 2008 task force on zero tolerance defined it as "a philosophy or policy that mandates the application of predetermined consequences, most often severe and punitive in nature, that are intended to be applied regardless of the gravity of behavior, mitigating circumstances, or situational context."[33] These policies—which echo the discriminatory and brutal federal and state mandatory minimum sentencing trends—are unconcerned with fairness by definition. Nor are they effective, the APA's task force found, at achieving *any* of their ostensible educational goals. Stemming in-school violence, increasing the consistency of discipline, creating a better learning environment for nondisruptive students, deterring further misbehavior, upping parent and community support for schools: The investigation found mixed or no evidence that zero tolerance has helped at all.

Zero tolerance imagines that kids are at risk of being victimized (violence, drugs, general hooliganism), but it also imagines kids *as* risks to the school and other students. The APA's research found that zero-tolerance school policing "affected the delicate balance between the educational and juvenile justice systems, in particular, increasing schools' use of and reliance on strategies such as security technology, security personnel, and profiling, especially in high-minority, high-poverty school districts."[34] Children — black, indigenous, and Latinx children in particular — are overpoliced, especially within schools (more on this later). When it comes to children's life chances, zero tolerance is a self-fulfilling prophecy: School authorities warn students that any deviant behavior on a child's part is irresponsible because it could have severe and long-lasting consequences for their future, and then they enforce unreasonably harsh disciplinary standards that have severe and long-lasting consequences for the child's future. That's not a warning, it's a promise.

Even if parents and the government alike are taking an overactive interest in American children's progress into adulthood, how can we be sure that this isn't just affection gone too far? What distinguishes the way a caring family or state institution treats a child from the way an investor would, if they're both primarily concerned with the child's future success? An investor may want an asset to achieve its full potential, but the investor doesn't particularly care whether that kid is happy while they do it. A caring parent, on the other hand, balances an interest in a child's future achievement with the child's present wellbeing. If the changes in childhood over the past decades have really been made "with the interests of all children in mind," as the Harley Avenue letter said, then they should, at the very least, not be actively making children unhappier. Evidence, however, suggests that even this small hope is in vain.

1.5 Xtremely Sad Teens

A 2003 study by Mihaly Csikszentmihalyi and Jeremy Hunter published in the *Journal of Happiness Studies* used what the authors called the Experience Sampling Method (ESM), in which they equipped subjects with electronic pagers that would go off at random times during the subjects' waking week. At the buzz, the subjects would record their activity and relative happiness, as well as various other qualitative and quantitative information that spoke to what they were doing and their feelings about it. Their sample group was a race-, gender-, and class-diverse group of 828 students spread among the sixth, eighth, tenth, and twelfth grades. The report is filled with observations that probably wouldn't surprise too many teenagers:

The first part of the day, spent at work or school, tends to be less happy, except for a peak at lunch-time. There is a dip after lunch, followed by higher reports of happiness in the afternoon when one is again free...

Whenever students are involved with school-related activities, their happiness level is below average...

Young people are much happier in the afternoons and evenings of weekdays, when they are free of requirements imposed by adults, and on weekends. But by the end of the weekend, on

Sunday afternoons, their happiness decreases in anticipation of the school-day to come.[35]

There is a solid correlation between the unhappiness teens report experiencing during an activity in the Csikszentmihalyi and Hunter study and the increase in time children reported spending on an activity in the Hoffreth time diaries referenced earlier in this chapter. To put it simply: American kids and teens, across race, gender, and class lines, are spending less time doing things that make them happy (like self-directed play with their friends and eating—pretty much the only two activities they report enjoying) and more time doing things that make them especially unhappy (like homework and listening to lectures).

After an exhaustive study of school shootings, journalist Mark Ames concluded that "Kids are demonstrably more miserable today than they used to be."[36] What Ames found, to his surprise, was that other students expressed sympathy and understanding for shooters. In his investigations into individual incidents in the 1980s, 1990s, and early 2000s collected in the book *Going Postal: Rage, Murder, and Rebellion: From Reagan's Workplaces to Clinton's Columbine and Beyond,* Ames found that, contrary to media depictions, kids—including the shooters—understood the target of these attacks to be the immiserating school itself, rather than a particular bully or clique of classmates. It's this anger and misery at the ever-tightening restrictions on their daily lives that kids can empathize with, and Ames is right to categorize acts of school violence with workplace violence. As we'll see, trends in youth anxiety and depression support the idea that American kids are significantly less happy than they have been in previous generations, which follows logically from their spending more of their time doing things that make them unhappy and less of it on the few things that even teens enjoy.

1.6 I Guess This Is Growing Up

In the traditional—though relatively recent—model of modern Western childhood, kids' activity isn't work. There's no surplus from their product for the owners to confiscate, so they can't possibly be doing labor in the way that wage laborers do. But by looking at children as investments, we can see where the product of children's labor is stored: in the machine-self, in their human capital. Under this framework, it's a kid's job to stay eligible for the labor market (not in jail, not insane, and not dead—which is more work for some than others), and any work product beyond that adds to their résumé. If more human capital automatically led to a higher standard of living, this model could be the foundation for an American meritocracy. But Millennials' extra work hasn't earned them the promised higher standard of living. By every metric, this generation is the most educated in American history, yet Millennials are worse off economically than their parents, grandparents, and even great-grandparents. Every authority from moms to presidents told Millennials to accumulate as much human capital as we could, and we did, but the market hasn't held up its side of the bargain. What gives? And why did we make this bargain in the first place?

As it turns out, just because you can produce an unprecedented amount of value doesn't necessarily mean you can feed yourself under twenty-first-century American capitalism. Kids spend their childhoods investing the only thing they have: their effort, their attention, their days and nights, their labor-time. (And, if they're lucky, a large chunk of whatever money their parents have.) If the purpose of all this labor, all the lost play, all the hours doing unpleasant tasks *isn't* to ensure a good life for the kids doing the work and being invested in, if it isn't in the "interests of all children," then what is it for? Whose interests is it in if not our own? To find out, we have to look at what happens to kids when we start growing up.

America doesn't actually prepare every child for college, but if you pick any individual kid and ask any mainstream adult authority what they should do with the next part of their life, I'd bet $30,000 at 7 percent interest that the advice includes enrolling in higher education of some sort. As the only sanctioned game in town, college admission becomes a well-structured, high-stakes simulation of a worker's entry into the labor market. Applicants inventory their achievements, careful not to undercount by a drop, and present them in the most attractive package possible. College admissions are the "boss" of aspirational childhood, in the video game sense: They're the final hard test, the one everything else was a preparation for, the one that determines what comes next. The admissions officers are also the boss, insofar as they are the ones who evaluate kids' work, who decide how much all their labor, all their *self*, is worth.

Using the data carefully and anxiously prepared by millions of kids about the human capital they've accumulated over the previous eighteen years, higher education institutions make decisions: collectively evaluating, accepting, and cutting hopeful children in tranches like collateralized debt obligations that are then sorted among the institutions according to their own rankings (for which they compete aggressively, of course). It is not the first time children are weighed, but it is the most comprehensive and often the most directly consequential. College admissions offices are the rating agencies for kids, and once the kid-bond is rated, it has four or so years until it's expected to produce a return. And those four years are expensive.

Chapter Two

Go to College

Uncle Ben: Look, we throw a lot of fancy words in front of these
kids in order to attract them to going to school in the belief that
they're gonna have a better life, and we know that all we were
doing is breeding a whole new generation of buyers and sellers...and indoctrinating them into a lifelong hell of debt and
indecision!

Jack: I...I, I just don't understand.

Uncle Ben: DO I HAVE TO SPOON FEED IT TO YA? Look,
there's only one reason that kids want to go to school.

Jack: Which is?

Uncle Ben: ...To get a good job...To get a good job, with a great
starting salary.

—Accepted *(2006)*

You can't talk about contemporary higher education without talking
about money, which is fine, because only fools are even tempted to
try. Between 1979 and 2014, the price of tuition and fees at four-year
nonprofit US colleges, adjusted for inflation, has jumped 197 percent
at private schools and 280 percent at public ones, accelerating faster
than housing prices or the cost of medical care or really anything you
could compare it to except maybe oil.[1]

But while college applicants' faith in the value of higher education
has only increased—at least in terms of what they're willing to pay

and how much debt they're willing to take on—employers' has declined. Wages for college-educated workers outside of the inflated finance industry have stagnated or diminished, with real wages for young graduates down 8.5 percent between 2000 and 2012.[2] Un- and underemployment have hit recent graduates especially hard, nearly doubling post-2007.[3] The result is that the most indebted generation in history is without the dependable jobs it needs to escape. And like the debt, these facts about the state of higher education are inescapable. Regardless of whether or not any particular parent or guidance counselor is doing the right thing by advising any individual child to prepare for, apply to, or take out loans to attend college, these are the aggregate effects of treating higher education the way America does.

In the video game that is American childhood, higher education isn't the final boss, after all—it's more like the beginning of a new level.

2.1 The Average Student

When you hear "college student," what do you picture? Maybe it's a frat party, with backward hats and kegs of cheap beer and lots of loud noise. Maybe it's a seminar room full of students debating the finer points of Plato. Maybe it's a rowdy tailgate at a football game or a protest about safe spaces or glasses of fancy wine in an Ivy League secret society. The college student implied by Millennial childhood norms is overprotected to the point of permanent adolescence, but not many people are actually like that. We have a lot of college student media stereotypes, and many Americans have firm ideas about those kids and their various affectations. But that's not really what this chapter is about. What's more important is actual college students and the structures that subsume them.

There are some important myths to dispel: The average college student does not live on campus—only around 15 percent of undergraduates do. Most do not attend selective institutions that accept fewer than half of their applicants.[4] Only 19 percent of full-time undergraduates in four-year public degree programs graduate on time, and it's 5 percent for two-year programs.[5] Students from poor families who go to college will probably remain working-class—38 percent of people from low-income families will remain in the bottom two deciles regardless of their educational accomplishment. But the biggest myth is probably the one about students and wage labor.

In her book *Paying the Price,* Sara Goldrick-Rab (herself a scholar of education policy) writes about how she assumed that a drowsy student of hers had been partying too hard and failing to take her studies seriously. When Goldrick-Rab confronted the student, the professor learned a valuable lesson: The student had been working nights at the local grocery store because the graveyard shift paid a little better. She had been attending class after an 11-p.m.-to-6-a.m. shift, taking her education *very* seriously. This is a good example of the difference between college student stereotypes and the reality, and the experience prompted Goldrick-Rab to take a look at how hard students are working outside the classroom:

> Times have changed. In 1960, 25 percent of full-time college students between the ages of sixteen and twenty-four worked while enrolled. Five decades later, national statistics show that over 70 percent of undergraduates are working.... Twenty percent of all undergraduate students are employed full time, year-round. Among those working part time (52 percent of all students), half work more than twenty hours a week (26 percent of all students).[6]

In a study of scholarship students at public colleges in Wisconsin conducted by Goldrick-Rab, 23 percent of respondents in their second year of school worked between the hours of 10 p.m. and 8 a.m. For all the jokes about students living off ramen, undergraduates are significantly more likely to experience high levels of food insecurity (in technical terms: "hunger") than to live in a dorm.[7] Millennials have changed what it means to be a college student in practice, but the American "Town vs. Gown" imaginary hasn't been updated.

When I write about college students in this section, I'm not talking about a rarefied slice of the upper class, the scions of the rich and the famous. College students are regular people—mostly regular *workers*—who spend part of their work-time on their own human capital, like they've been told to. They are doing the work we all need them to do if this country and its economy are to have the trained workers they require to function and grow. The policies that affect college students affect all Americans, and looking forward, employers and policymakers alike are betting on near-universal higher education. The big question then is how the average student pays for it.

The prevailing logic is that investments in one's own working credentials are almost always good investments. Whatever you take out in student loans will come back to you in the form of higher wages down the line. And if they don't, you probably just need more education. There's no such thing as too much. The problem then becomes access to the cash in hand to invest in yourself or your child, rather than what higher education could cost, or how the market values degrees when more people have them. Debt is a bridge over the gap.

But what kinds of incentives motivate lenders to continue awarding loans for tens of thousands of dollars to teenagers facing both the worst youth unemployment rate in decades and an increasingly competitive global workforce? Why do universities need so much more money from students and their families? Where does the money come from, where does it go, and why does everyone keep insisting college is a good investment no matter what it costs?

2.2 Anyone Can Afford a Brand-New Diploma

Looking at the consistent patterns of higher education debt, it's hard to imagine that the federal government nationalized the vast majority of student lending—around 85 percent—in 2010.[8] Ever frightened of being labeled socialist, the Obama administration downplayed a cost offset in the 2010 Affordable Care Act that authorized the federal government to buy out most of the student loan industry. But since then, it's the feds who run the lending system directly, and the trillion-plus in student debt that the state holds makes up a plurality of its financial assets—37 percent, far more than national reserves officially hold in gold or foreign currency. Nationalizing around $850 million in outstanding debt and $100 billion in annual loan disbursement and cutting out private competitors is theoretically controversial, but by posing it as a debt-reducing cost offset, the Obama administration successfully reframed the move as a concession to Congressional Republicans. (Basically, since taking the place of private lenders saved the government money, by tacking it onto the ACA the administration reduced Obamacare's overall costs, which Republicans could hardly oppose.) Democrats, who don't want people to think of the welfare state as the home of Obamacare and student loans, were happy not to hype the state's new debt holdings.

Before the Obama administration's reform, most student lending was done through the ill-advised Federal Family Education Loan

(FFEL) Program, under which the federal government backed an intricate private system of dispersed lending agencies at a totally unnecessary cost to taxpayers. There was no sense in the government using its credit rating to support private lenders while the fat cats profited off students. From an accounting perspective it's a no-brainer: All they did was cut out the middleman. Not even the banks themselves could claim they were necessary, and every major private bank except Wells Fargo quietly exited the student loan industry entirely. But the government didn't know just how well their plan was going to work, how much money they were really going to save.

While economic recovery has been just around the corner for years—or so we're told—Treasury rates (the interest rates the government pays to borrow money) are still low, which has produced some unforeseen consequences for the federal government's takeover of the student loan industry. Because the government's borrowing costs are so low, student lending is incredibly profitable. The Department of Education expects to reap $18.99 in profit on every $100 in loans originated in 2014. Multiply that by 140 billion and we're talking over $25 billion in projected negative subsidy—that is, profit— off the 2014 cohort alone.[9] That is the current financial foundation for the American higher education system, but we don't like to talk about it that much.

When policymakers and commentators talk about the cost of higher education, they tend to frame it in terms of making it easier to attend college. In his 2014 State of the Union address, for example, President Obama mentioned college access four times, and he went so far as to suggest that every American needs postsecondary training of some sort to remain competitive on the labor market. Despite this rhetorical commitment to spreading the benefits of college, average student debt continued increasing under the Obama administration, from \$23,200 in 2008 to \$28,400 in 2013.[10, 11] Nationalization of the debt system certainly hasn't made higher education *cheaper*.

But as anyone who's seen an infomercial knows, affordability isn't just about cost, it's about the repayment terms. Paying \$1,800 for a Bowflex up front may cost about the same as eighteen payments of \$99.95, but it's a lot less affordable. When President Obama said in the State of the Union speech, "We worked with lenders to reform student loans, and today, more young people are earning college degrees than ever before," it sounded like there was a certain causal connection, as if reform had led to a reduction in the higher education debt burden that had freed up more young people to go to college. The reality is closer to the opposite: The more debt there is available, the more "affordable" college is. Washington's program for higher education accessibility isn't based on the "No one turned away for lack of funds" logic of a punk show at a Unitarian church; it's closer to "At no money down, anyone can get behind the wheel of a brand-new Mustang." This is how the president can call an escalation in average student debt an achievement in accessibility.

What happened? Even if the ideals of public education always have been glossy propaganda for investment in the upper ranks of the national labor force — a training school for bosses — at least it was an investment. This looks like a goofy scheme to stimulate consumer demand by dragging value from the future and spending it in the present. Recent high school graduates are the least creditworthy adults you can imagine; it's perfectly reasonable for Millennials to ask, "Why are they giving us all this money in the first place?" To answer that, we need to look at where the money is going.

The broad Washington policy consensus boils down to the idea that we need more college access, which means more debt. But the problem with student debt isn't that there's not enough of it, it's that American higher education costs too much. No mystification can disguise what anyone who can read a price tag already knows. But we ignore the cost because we're so dedicated to the axiomatic virtue of "College for all" that we consider a college education priceless. A hard look at young America means a hard look at what higher education has become, putting aside whatever sentimental attachments we might have to humanities seminars, poetry slams, or March Madness.

Higher education is, in addition to other things, an economic regime that extracts increasingly absurd amounts of money from millions of young people's as-yet-unperformed labor. For anyone who takes out a student loan—and that's two-thirds of students—succeeding at contemporary American childhood now means contracting out hours, days, years of their future work to the government, with no way to escape the consequences of what is barely a decision in the first place.

2.3 Why Is College So Expensive?

Why has the cost of education gone up so high so fast? In theory, the vast higher education public option should keep fees down across the board. Since the government holds a compelling interest in educating the population, it created a whole network of institutions, from two-year community colleges to the so-called Public Ivies like UC Berkeley and the University of Michigan at Ann Arbor. If these schools are reasonable substitutes for private schools, and they keep their costs in line with the actual expense of providing services, then the whole industry should hew to a cost curve that has less to do with demand than with necessary expenditures. Or so the theory goes.

Since almost all colleges are nonprofits, we assume people work in higher education for reasons other than financial gain, whether it be commitment to teaching the next generation, a passion for contributing to the sum of human knowledge and understanding, fear of social life outside the academy, or some combination of all three. The bottom line is that on some level we expect that institutions of higher education will act in the interest of students, at least more than private companies motivated by profit would. But even though we assume something akin to custodial behavior from colleges and universities, it's still reasonable to ask what this consistent escalation in costs is for.

First, let's look at where the money hasn't gone: instruction. As Marc Bousquet, a leading researcher into the changing structures of higher education, wrote in *How the University Works:*

> If you're enrolled in four college classes right now, you have a pretty good chance that one of the four will be taught by someone who has earned a doctorate and whose teaching, scholarship, and service to the profession has undergone the intensive peer scrutiny associated with the tenure system. In your other three classes, however, you are likely to be taught by someone who has started a degree but not finished it; was hired by a manager, not professional peers; may never publish in the field she is teaching; got into the pool of persons being considered for the job because she was willing to work for wages around the official poverty line (often under the delusion that she could "work her way into" a tenurable position); and does not plan to be working at your institution three years from now.[12]

Fewer than forty years ago, when the explosive growth in tuition began, these proportions were reversed. Graduate students are highly represented among this new precarious class of teachers; with so much debt available to them, universities can force them to scrape by on sub-minimum-wage fellowships, which makes grad students a great source of cheap instructional labor. There are fewer tenure-track jobs available (as a proportion), which means that recent PhDs, themselves often overwhelmed with debt, have little choice but to accept insecure adjunct positions while their wages are depressed by the next crop of graduate student workers. It's a dizzying cycle, but university administrators like the ride: They hired part-time faculty at 2.6 times the rate of full-time between 1990 and 2012.[13] Rather than producing a better-trained, more professional teaching corps, increased tuition and debt have enabled the opposite. So who's reaping the rewards?

If overfed teachers aren't the causes or beneficiaries of higher tuition (as they're so often depicted), then perhaps it's worth looking up the food chain. As faculty jobs have become increasingly contingent and precarious, administration has become less so. Formerly, administrators were more or less teachers with added responsibilities; nowadays, they function more like standard corporate managers or nonprofit fundraisers—and they're paid like them too. Once a few entrepreneurial schools made this switch, market pressures compelled the rest to follow the revenue-prioritizing model, which leads directly to high salaries for in-demand administrators. Even at nonprofit schools, top-level administrators and financial managers pull down high-six- and even seven-figure salaries, closer to their industry counterparts than their fellow faculty members. And while the proportion of tenure-track teaching faculty has dwindled, the number of managers has jumped in both relative and absolute terms.[14] A bigger administration also consumes a larger portion of available funds, so it's unsurprising that budget share for instruction has dipped.

When you hire corporate managers, you get managed like a corporation, and the race for tuition dollars and grants from government and private partnerships has become the driving objective of the contemporary university administration. The goal for large state universities and elite private colleges alike has ceased to be (if it ever was) building well-educated citizens; now they hardly even bother to prepare students to assume their places among the ruling class. Instead, we have, in Bousquet's words, "the entrepreneurial urges, vanity, and hobbyhorses of administrators: Digitize the curriculum! Build the best pool/golf course/stadium in the state! Bring more souls to God! Win the all-conference championship!"[15] These expensive projects are all part of another cycle: Corporate universities must be competitive in recruiting students who are already set up to become rich alumni, so they have to spend on attractive extras, which means they need more revenue, so they need more students paying higher tuition. For-profits aren't the only ones consumed with selling product. And if a humanities program can't demonstrate its economic utility to its institution (which can't afford to haul "deadweight") and its students (who understand the need for marketable degrees), then it faces cuts, the preferred neoliberal management technique. Students apparently have received the message loud and clear, as "business" has quickly become the nation's most popular major by over 100 percent.[16]

The clearest description of why education costs are so high and where they're going comes from a whistle-blower of sorts. During the 2009 fight over a 32 percent increase in the price of tuition across the University of California system—a struggle that was valiantly fought and sadly lost—professor Bob Meister of UC Santa Cruz released a public letter called "They Pledged Your Tuition" designed to clarify what exactly the UC schools were doing with the fees. A professor of social and political thought, Meister went against the prevailing faculty wisdom—namely that all money problems in public higher education are the result of state divestment in higher education — and blamed the out-of-control growth of bond-financed capital projects.

Meister wrote that because state money can't be used to finance construction bonds (by law), UC management had pledged future tuition hikes to satisfy bond-rating agencies, allowing the schools to continue to borrow money at low rates to build a new stadium in Berkeley, a new coffeehouse in Davis, a new campus police station in Los Angeles, and more:

> Construction funding is a reason why the Regents want to raise tuition, perhaps the most important reason, but, as students, you are unlikely to go along with big increases to fund UC's list of construction projects. Cutting back on instructional budgets is how they get you to agree to higher tuition without telling you how much will go to fund construction. On my campus, the most visible instructional cuts typically become permanent, and we're told that without higher tuition they would have been worse. Campus administrations can *always* say that no particular tuition increase is ever *large enough* to reverse whatever instructional cuts were imposed to persuade you that it was necessary. If you accept this claim, you'll never question how much of your tuition is used to fund construction, and whether you would have found an increase justified had you known.[17]

The policy debate around higher education costs tends to distinguish between public and private institutions, but evidence suggests the two are marching upward to the beat of the same drum. Over the past thirty years, costs of attendance (tuition, fees, room and board) in real terms have risen around 220 percent at *both* public and private four-year institutions (219 and 223 percent, respectively).[18] The ratio between the two has remained constant. It would be one hell of a coincidence if private and public universities responded to entirely different sets of cost pressures in *the same way* over the course of *three decades*. The most obvious explanation is that nonprofit higher education has become a single industry with premium and generic brands. If you don't believe me, then at least believe the financial services agency Moody's, whose 2013 report describes the distinction in the clear and unashamed language of unaccountable finance professionals: "Public universities are now as market driven as private universities, but remain a lower cost option with stronger pricing power."[19]

In the standard liberal narrative, public higher education is getting worse and more expensive at the same time because subsidies from state governments and the federal government (in the form of Pell Grants) have decreased, pushing the cost burden onto students and their families. The solution, according to this diagnosis, is increased state support for public universities. The evidence, however, doesn't back up this story. Though there has been some decrease in state support since the 2008 crisis, the past thirty years do not show a withdrawal of state funds commensurate with the rise in costs to students. But if we can cease to imagine that the higher education industry is an oasis of care and concern in our vast desert of market indifference — which, quite frankly, only a deluded few employed in the industry believe anyway — then we might be emotionally prepared to look at higher education using the financial system's heartless analytics, which explain perfectly well why costs have risen.

Higher education managers have one set of answers for the public, but the bromides about the lifelong value of a college education don't work on the bond market. In 2013, Moody's issued a negative outlook rating for the US higher education sector, suggesting that schools were, in aggregate, not a good investment. The first reason these analysts give is that schools have more or less hit the ceiling when it comes to charging families for higher education.[20] Let that sink in for a second: Investors who have no particular interest in the wellbeing of families, investors doing fully rationalized analysis — these investors thought schools were charging *as much as they possibly could* in tuition.

Here's how Moody's described the current state of public education pricing in November of 2013, in the wake of 2008:

> For several years, lower sticker prices allowed public universities to increase tuition at extraordinary rates in order to compensate for declining state appropriations. While some universities retain pricing power, it can be constrained by either mission-based or political limitations on tuition increases.
>
> As a result, public universities are increasingly competing for out-of-state students, including those from outside of the US, for which the universities can often raise tuition at a greater rate.[21]

The competition for high-value customers and research grant money has pressured schools to invest in "capital, information systems, faculty compensation and program renewal" at a time when they have seemingly few options for increasing cash flow.[22] During good years schools built and innovated and paid expensive consultants to do dozens of different things; now they're stuck in a totally unsustainable model, and the only way out — at least judging from the way college administrators are behaving — is to try to climb over all the other crabs to the top of the *U.S. News & World Report*–ranked bucket.

A 2014 report from the Delta Cost Project at the American Institutes for Research (the party people at the AIR had some fun and named it "Labor Intensive or Labor Expensive?") found that between 2000 and 2012, the nonprofit private and public higher education workforce rose 28 percent. "The higher education workforce—from tenured professors to part-time adjuncts, and from executives and professionals to support staff—is changing rapidly," the report says, and the numbers agree.[23] Careful readers might wonder if the jump in the higher education workforce mirrors the increase in enrollment over the same period, and it does. But the question isn't how *many* employees colleges have added, but *which kind*.

Changes in the composition of the higher education workforce are a good way to track the ways colleges have shifted their focus, since labor costs amount to 75 percent of university expenditures on average.[24] If schools were responding to higher enrollment by hiring lots of new tenure-track faculty, that would indicate one thing about their management vision, whereas a declining share of spending for instruction would indicate another. It's the latter we've seen, as the report reveals that a small number of pricey professors—for whom universities compete aggressively—have received large salary bumps, while the overall cost per instructor and share of budget for instruction have declined. This is another instance of the winner-take-all tendency, where a small cohort of scholars garner all the right credentials and enough celebrity to leave the rest in the dust.

Between 1990 and 2012, the head count of nonprofessional campus workers—technical, clerical, skilled craft, and service/maintenance—declined sharply as schools invested in automation. The number of part-time faculty overtook the number of full-time faculty between 1990 and 2000 in private and public sectors.[25] Universities have benefitted from automating solid jobs that don't require college degrees, and at the same time they've lowered the quality of the instructor jobs that *do* require degrees. The university, as we will come to see in the next chapter, is at the forefront of advancements in labor efficiency, but that hasn't meant improved learning conditions.

The AIR report found that universities have been hiring professional workers — business analysts, human resources staff, admissions staff, etc. — at the highest rate, exceeding the rate at which enrollment increased. The report describes the growth in this sector:

> The explosion of new workers attending to the noninstructional side of higher education has not gone unnoticed on college and university campuses. Although the most visible positions — such as newly hired executives, managers, and administrators — tend to draw the greatest attention, most hiring has occurred within the administrative offices they often oversee. Professional employees — such as business analysts, human resources staff, admissions staff, computer administrators, counselors, athletic staff, and health workers — are the largest group of noninstructional staff on campus. These positions typically either support the business functions of colleges and universities or provide noninstructional services to students.[26]

All types of private and public nonprofit colleges have added these kinds of professional staffers while increasing reliance on part-time instructors. To the high degree that this has occurred, universities have deprioritized education and prioritized business administration. The consequences as I detail them in this chapter have been the natural and predictable outcomes.

What this all amounts to is a clear tendency for both public and private colleges to behave like businesses, passing off a lower-quality product at a higher price by tacking on highly leveraged shiny extras unrelated to the core educational mission. Stadium skyboxes, flat-screen monitors, marble floors, and hors d'oeuvres for the alumni association. Consultants of all flavors and salaried employees to make sure it's all efficient. Competition hasn't improved the quality of higher education, it has made colleges more like sleepaway camps or expensive resorts, cruise ships with lucrative fast-food concessions and bookstores full of branded tchotchkes for sale.

2.4 Failing Reform School

With young Americans consistently ranking student loans among their biggest concerns—and with economists scared that five-figure debts will depress consumer spending—you might expect there would be some substantial reform proposals on the table. You would be sadly mistaken. Rather, policymakers have treated higher education costs like a public relations problem. There's no way to address the underlying issue of too many young Americans owing too much in student debt without the lender (the United States government, in most cases) taking a hit. But neither the administration nor the Congressional leadership of either big party has shown any appetite for taking major steps to even reduce the state's profits.

While escalating student debt makes headlines, the federal government is understandably embarrassed about raking in more profits than Exxon. Senator Elizabeth Warren has made student loan profits a national issue. "It's time to end the practice of profiting from young people who are trying to get an education and refinance existing loans," Warren said in a January 2014 statement.[27] Though she's right to draw attention to a particularly egregious symptom (the profits), a January 2014 report from the Government Accountability Office

(GAO) highlights how deep the problems with the student lending structure go.

Senator Warren's hope has been that the government could set borrower interest rates in advance to precisely and consistently balance federal revenues and costs. This was a hope the GAO quickly dashed in their report, helpfully titled "Borrower Interest Rates Cannot Be Set in Advance to Precisely and Consistently Balance Federal Revenues and Costs."[28] It's the oldest play in the book when it comes to pretending to address an intractable policy issue: Commission a report that says it's not feasible to do anything at all.

The report was ostensibly a response to H.R. 1911 — the Bipartisan Student Loan Certainty Act of 2013. Congress and the administration fought long and hard over this bill, which sets interest rates on direct loans for three different loan categories in perpetuity. As the Department of Education tried to figure out how to become the nation's largest student lender, they were pressed for time by student loan interest rates that were set to double — the result of the last time Congress negotiated a quick fix. While factions offered six various proposals, the deadline lapsed and borrower rates did double.[29] Luckily, this lender doesn't just make its own laws, it makes its own time too; when Congress finally agreed on the bill, they made it retroactive. The bill they ended up with looked most like the proposal from Republican Representative John Kline, which was found to *generate* revenue: $3.7 billion, to be exact.[30] That the ultimate (revenue-neutral) resolution was worse for borrowers than the most conservative plan on offer points to how little daylight there is between the major parties on this issue.

In return for slightly higher interest rates than the president had proposed, the Obama administration won a new repayment program called Pay As You Earn (PAYE). This provision is an improvement on the complicated and rarely used Income-Based Repayment (IBR) program that existed previously. Under PAYE, new borrowers who opt in can cap their payments at 10 percent of their discretionary income, and after twenty years of on-time monthly installments and annual income reports, their loans will be forgiven. It sounds almost like a real answer to the student debt crisis, but the numbers don't bear that out.

At no point in the White House press release is there a reference to how much money the program expects to save student debtors as a whole.[31] That's because it doesn't save them any. Not only does the government's own student aid site admit that PAYE will most likely cause enrollees to pay more interest over time, the Obama administration brags that the program won't cost taxpayers a dime.[32] Since there's nowhere else for the money to come from, that means that if there are any borrowers getting a break on their overall payments, it's because another borrower is paying for it with higher interest rates. The number are revealing: The Congressional Budget Office estimated that opening PAYE to all borrowers would cost the government a near-term total $3.6 billion, a near-even trade for the $3.7 billion revenue in the GOP's interest rate proposal.[33] The Student Loan Certainty Act was a good deal for both sides: The Obama administration and the Democrats got an accomplishment in PAYE, and the GOP got a revenue-neutral bill. It's an expert reshuffling that makes it look like a problem is being addressed, while sweeping the issue of student debt under the sofa to deal with later.

The White House press release on PAYE was titled "We Can't Wait," but the opposite is true: The DoE can and will wait decades for borrowers to pay back their loans. The *New York Times* ran the numbers on PAYE compared to standard repayment for the median borrower and found that PAYE actually costs over $3,000 more over the life of the loan, for one simple reason:[34] longer repayment periods mean more interest. Not only do these reforms not address the scale of the problem, they're not even reforms at all insofar as "reform" is supposed to mean a good-faith effort to solve a problem. The only problem student loan reform exists to solve is the perception that the government isn't doing anything to solve the student loan crisis. And that perception is well founded in reality.

2.5 When Is a Default Not a Default?

Risk of massive student loan default looms large in the American public imagination. Since the 2008 mortgage crisis, many commentators — myself included at one point — have likened the escalating mass of student debt and its derivative financial products to the housing bubble. The idea is that if a bunch of borrowers couldn't pay all at once and the quality of their loans had to be downgraded, it would be a disaster. Given what we know — over a trillion dollars' worth of outstanding student loan debt and the increasing scarcity of jobs that will put borrowers in a position to pay that money back quickly — that scenario doesn't sound farfetched. To test the likelihood that a wave of defaults could put the government on the hook for serious costs down the line, the GAO projected a scenario in which the portion of total loans in the highest risk category went from 6.7 percent to 51.2 percent. That's a huge swing, a nightmare in the conventional wisdom. What lender wouldn't be concerned if over half their loans were suddenly super-high-risk? The federal government, it turns out. The GAO estimated that, compared to change in the underlying variable, the risk would have almost no effect on the lending program's costs, tiny compared even to low-risk income-based repayment.[35] Why doesn't it worry the government when student borrowers threaten to default on their loans?

Defaulted student loans don't just disappear into a government loss column—in fact, they don't disappear anywhere. The idea of defaulting implies that the debtor is unable to, and therefore does not, pay off the loan. But that's not how it works. At the time of this writing, the latest numbers are for loans issued in Fiscal Year 2014: The government expects to make a staggering $140 billion in student loans,[36] of which around 17.5 percent are projected to default at some point in the future.[37]

During the mortgage crisis, homeowners who found themselves with negative equity (owing more on their houses than the houses were worth) could walk away. Students aren't as lucky: Graduates can't ditch their degrees, even if they borrowed more money than their résumé can command on the market. Americans overwhelmed with normal consumer debt (like credit cards) have the option of bankruptcy, and although it's an arduous and credit-score-killing process, it's a way out. But students don't have that option. Before 2005, students could use bankruptcy to escape education loans that weren't provided directly by the federal government, but the facetiously named Bankruptcy Abuse Prevention and Consumer Protection Act extended nondischargeability to all education loans, even credit cards used to pay school bills.

Today, student debt is an exceptionally punishing kind of debt to have. Not only is it very hard to escape through bankruptcy, but student loans have no expiration date and collectors can garnish wages, Social Security payments, and even unemployment benefits. When someone like *Vox*'s Dylan Matthews writes that the government is "better at making collections than private lenders," it sounds like he's talking about economies of scale.[38] But the government is more like a loan shark who can make riskier investments than private lenders can because he has ways of collecting from delinquent borrowers that are not on the menu for other lenders.

The Mafia aren't the only lenders who make their own rules. Through the use of its own special set of compliance tools—particularly wage garnishment, something not available to any other lender—the federal government has tied student loan repayment very closely to the continued functioning of the US economy. As long as enough college-educated workers survive to work more and make wages that can be garnisheed, they will pay their loans. And the Treasury doesn't need borrowers to hurry on repayment as long as they can count on getting the money back someday. These conditions make student loans effectively just as safe as Treasury bills, which are themselves low-risk investments in the continued expansion of American production. That's why the average defaulted student borrower still ends up paying the Treasury more than 100 percent of their loan's principal.[39] Student loan default does not, on average, exist.

2.6 The Student Debt Time Machine

Here's where we are now: All American children are told to exercise self-discipline and spend the only things they have (their time and effort) working and competing for a spot in a college freshman class. If they're lucky enough to achieve this goal, they'll borrow on average tens of thousands of dollars from the government for an increasingly diluted education. Schools take this $100+ billion a year in government money, backed by their students' ability to do work in the future, and spend it like their job is to produce more spending. Colleges have dug themselves so deep into their shining marble pit that not even the vultures in the bond market want much to do with them. Meanwhile, debtors can't walk away from student loans unless they can walk away from themselves.

Even if it were larger, the subprime housing market is a less sophisticated and stable way to gin up demand than the student debt industrial complex. People can't default on their human capital, even if it's overleveraged. That means that as long as the government keeps treating student loans as a special type of practically inalienable debt, when this value is created, it's created for real. Student debt is a kind of time travel for value: Borrowers take out loans based on the idea that the returns on a college education will always exceed the costs, and they're made to pay regardless.

Here's how the time machine works: Say you—hypothetically—need to generate demand for a bunch of construction projects (a state-of-the-art athletic facility, perhaps, or a new performing arts center designed by a famous architect) because the housing market collapsed. You look high and low, and everyone is tapped out. It's a bad economy. But you're smart, and you know money is more complicated than that. Just because the demand doesn't exist *now* doesn't mean it won't exist *later,* and if it exists *later,* then making it appear now is just a matter of the right forecasts and the right lender with the right interest rates. You don't want another bubble, though, so you need to anchor these predictions to something that can't evaporate if market conditions change. And if there's one thing you know about a future in which firms are able to collect debts, where we have to spend money to buy food and stay alive, it's that people will be working. Human capital is the present value of the one thing you know, in aggregate, has to happen in the future: Workers are going to work.

Of course, a national scheme in which young people pledge the product of their future labor for straight cash is suspect, and besides, who knows what kids might buy with their pockets full? They might not invest in large real estate projects, for one thing. But universities turn the paychecks of tomorrow into construction today. And because of the government's extraordinary collection abilities, there's no easy way for the value to disappear. If you're *really* sophisticated, you'll project future increases in the costs you can charge students, then go to the bond market and get even *more* money to build stuff. When the government and nonprofit foundations and employers say we need more kids in college, part of what they're saying is that we need to mine more value from the future and spend it in the present, even if they don't think of it that way.

But what kind of labor market do borrowers enter with these loans? When the bill comes due, what kind of position are they in to repay, and can they make a life for themselves at the same time? And what about the kids who aren't "properly equipped" for the twenty-first-century job market, the ones who didn't go to college, or didn't go to the right one, or didn't graduate? Getting into college is the first big test of what a kid's human capital is worth, but college itself is at best an opportunity for further investment. The job market is where the investments start yielding returns. Or not.

Chapter Three

Work (Sucks)

You can be a boss or you can get a job

—*Shy Glizzy, "Awwsome"*

There's a contradiction in the premise so far: On the one hand, every kid is supposed to spend their childhood readying themselves for a good job in the skills-based information economy. On the other hand, improvements in productive technology mean an overall decrease in labor costs. That means workers get paid a smaller portion of the value they create as their productivity increases. In aggregate, this operates like a bait and switch: Employers convince kids and their families to invest in training by holding out the promise of good jobs, while firms use this very same training to reduce labor costs. The better workers get, the more money and time we put into building up our human capital, the worse the jobs get. And that's a big problem because, as we've seen over the last two chapters, America is producing some damn good workers.

We've already seen a detailed and representative example of how the labor market has changed: the higher education sector. In Chapter 2, we looked over the Delta Cost Project study on the shifting composition of the higher education workforce. Universities have reduced the share of nonprofessional campus workers—jobs that largely did not require college education but still paid living wages—through costly investment in automation and digitization. The middle-income jobs that universities haven't been able to automate have been outsourced to for-profit contractors who can do a better job managing (read: keeping to a minimum) employee wages and benefits. The contractors will sometimes even pay for the privilege—as when Barnes & Noble takes over a campus bookstore or McDonald's a food court concession. On the classroom side, a glut of qualified graduates facing an unwelcoming job market has pushed down the cost of instruction labor. Graduate instructors and adjunct lecturers now teach the majority of college classes, and the tenured professor seems to be going extinct, with the title, security, perks, and pay scale reserved for a lucky few and the occasional hire whose fame extends beyond their subject field. At the top, salaries for administrators (and surgeons and athletic coaches) now reach into the millions, as they work to keep everyone else's compensation as low as possible.

Higher education is just one industry, and it follows—sometimes leads—the same trends as the rest of the labor market. But colleges aren't just shifting the composition of their own workforce; they're facilitating wider changes as well. Across the economy, bad jobs are getting worse, good jobs are getting better, and the middle is disappearing. University of North Carolina sociologist Arne L. Kalleberg calls this move "polarization." As Millennials enter the workforce, we've faced a set of conditions that are permanently different than what previous generations have experienced. As Kalleberg puts it:

> The growing gap between good- and bad-quality jobs is a long-term structural feature of the changing labor market. Polarized and precarious employment systems result from the economic restructuring and removal of institutional protections that have

been occurring since the 1970s; they are not merely temporary features of the business cycle that will self-correct once economic conditions improve. In particular, bad jobs are no longer vestigial but, rather, are a central—and in some cases growing—portion of employment in the United States.[1]

When older commentators compare the current labor market to past ones, they usually disguise the profound and lasting changes that have occurred over the past few decades. But when the elder generations set the stakes for childhood education and achievement as high as they do, they're being more honest: Where you end up on the job distribution map after all that time in school really *is* more important than it used to be. It's harder to compete for a good job, the bad jobs you can hope to fall back on are worse than they used to be, and both good and bad jobs are less secure. The intense anxiety that has overcome American childhood flows from a reasonable fear of un-, under-, and just plain lousy employment.

To see what roles young people are being readied to fill in twenty-first-century America, we need to understand changes in the job market over the period in question. Jobs are the way most Americans afford to live week after week, month after month, the way most parents can afford to raise children, and what we spend a lot of time preparing kids to do. Despite changing a lot over the past thirty to forty years, the relation between employers and workers still structures American lives. It controls not only the access to income, the ability to pay back educational debts, and the ability to rent a room, buy a house, or start a family, but also public goods like medical care and retirement support. We've put the reproduction of society in the hands of owners motivated purely by profit. As a result, the consequences of career success and failure are growing heavier as time goes on. Work is intensifying across the board, abetted by communications technology that erases the distinction between work-time and the rest of life. For young people entering or preparing to enter the labor market, these extraordinary developments have always been the way things are.

3.1 The Changing Character of Work

In his book-length report *Good Jobs, Bad Jobs,* Kalleberg takes a macroscopic view of changes in the American job market from the 1970s to the 2000s. (Because the study is such a strong and well-supported survey, I'll be referring to Kalleberg's summaries often throughout this chapter.) What he found is totally inconsistent with what's supposed to be labor's deal with the twenty-first century: The population gets more educated, more effective, better skilled, and in return, it's rewarded with high-paying postindustrial jobs. Instead, Kalleberg found the polarization mentioned above, as well as decreasing job security across both good and bad jobs. Despite all the preparatory work, all the new college degrees, all the investment in human capital, the rewards haven't kept up with the costs for most.

The growth of a "new economy" characterized by more knowledge-intensive work has been accompanied by the accelerated pace of technological innovation and the continued expansion of service industries as the principal sources of jobs. Political policies such as the replacement of welfare by workfare programs in the 1990s have made it essential for people to participate in paid employment at the same time that jobs have become more precarious.

The labor force has become more diverse, with marked increases in the number of women, non-white, older, and immigrant workers, and growing divides between people with different amounts of education. Ideological changes have supported these structural changes, with shifts toward greater individualism and personal accountability for work and life replacing notions of collective responsibility.[2]

Every bit of this so-called progress has made employees both desperately productive and productively desperate, while the profits from their labor accrue to a shrinking ownership class. From this perspective, all that work in childhood seems motivated more by fear of a lousy future than by hope for dignity, security, and leisure time. "Since both good jobs (for example, well-paid consultants) and bad jobs are generally insecure," Kalleberg writes, "it has become increasingly difficult to distinguish good and bad jobs on the basis of their degree of security."[3] Paying to train employees you might not need later is inefficient, and inefficiency is mismanagement. As a result, today's employers are scared of commitment. The inequality that results isn't cyclical—these aren't just temporary growing pains as workers adjust to market demand for new skills. It's the successful and continued development of a wage labor system in which owners always think of workers as just another cost to be reduced.

There are a lot of ways to talk about this dynamic, a lot of metrics and statistics and anecdotal data we could use to illustrate how most workers are living with less. Because the world of policy analysis doesn't have the tools to look at the comparative worsening conditions of people's everyday lives directly, each measure has its problems— but looking at each of them can help us glimpse the bigger picture.

3.2 Getting Paid

Take the question of wages: The category of wages doesn't include income derived from rents or investments. Hedge fund managers are fighting an ongoing battle to keep their astronomical compensation categorized as investment income instead of wages, to avoid taxes, and this also skews the distribution. Many low-wage jobs are off the books and don't show up in government data. Which is all to say, the richest and poorest Americans aren't represented in our wage measures. And yet, the numbers *still* show growing polarization and the evaporation of middle-income jobs.

The most important confounding variable when it comes to American labor compensation is gender. As social and educational barriers to women's participation in the workforce have eroded, firms have looked to women as a lower-wage alternative. Women still aren't paid as well as men for the same productivity, but the wage gap has closed significantly since the late 1970s. Even though the gap persists, its narrowing has a large effect on historical measures of compensation. When you don't separate the numbers by gender, the narrowing gender wage gap pushes the average wage up significantly, but that doesn't mean the quality of jobs has risen. Rather, it's an example of firms trying out new strategies to keep their costs down by growing the pool of available labor.

Even with those caveats in place, this is how Kalleberg describes the body of research on wages by quintile:

Wages have stagnated for most of the labor force since the 1970s, especially for men. Rates of real wage growth in the United States have averaged less than 1 percent per year since 1973.... Median wages for men (50th percentile) have remained stagnant, at nearly $18 per hour, while median wages for women have increased from $11.28 in 1973 to $14.55 in 2009. Wages for men in the twentieth percentile have fallen from almost $12 per hour in 1973 to $10 per hour in 2009; while wages for women in the lowest quintile have increased slightly, from about $8 per hour in 1973 to about $9 per hour in 2009.[4]

He calculated the relations between different deciles over time and found that the ratio between the bottom of the wage scale and the middle has been steady since the mid-1990s. The ratio between the top 10 percent and the median decile of wage earners, on the other hand, has consistently escalated over the same period. "It is the increase in jobs with very high wages — the top 10 percent, or even the top 1 or 5 percent," Kalleberg writes, " — that is primarily respon-

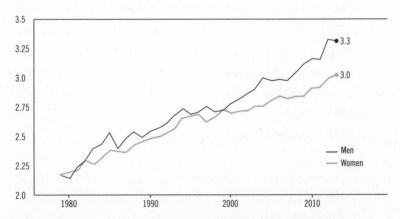

Wage Inequality Has Dramatically Increased Among Both Men and Women Over the Last 35 Years

Wage gap* between the 95th and 50th percentiles,** by gender, 1979–2013

* Ratio of workers' wages at the higher earnings percentile to workers' wages at the lower percentile.

** The xth-percentile wage is the wage at which x% of wage earners earn less and (100 − x)% earn more.

An Increasing Share of Men of Child-Rearing Age Earn Low Wages
Share of workers earning poverty-level hourly wages, by gender and age group,
1979 and 2013

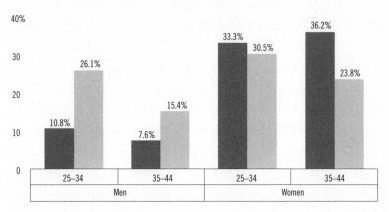

Note: The poverty-level wage in 2013 was $11.45.

sible for driving the overall increases in wage inequality in the United States since the mid- to late-1980s."[5] A report from the Economic Policy Institute (EPI) disaggregated inequality between the median wage earned and the ninety-fifth percentile by gender and found steady, nearly equal growth in inequality for both men and women.[6] That means inequality between male and female wage earners has narrowed overall, but inequality within each gender group has grown.

Another report from the EPI compared the Bureau of Labor Statistics' number of workers earning poverty-level wages in 1979 and 2013 as divided by age and gender.[7] In 1979, the relations between the numbers make sense for the late-ish twentieth century: 10.8 percent of male workers aged twenty-five to thirty-four and 7.6 percent of male workers aged thirty-five to forty-four worked at or under the poverty line. On the women's side, the age gap was the same size but in the other direction: one-third of younger women workers worked for poverty wages in 1979, compared to 36.2 percent of older women.

This reflects the larger proportion of women moving into higher-paid skilled jobs. But by 2013, younger workers were at a very serious disadvantage: The age gap for male workers more than tripled, with 26.1 percent of younger and 15.4 percent of older male workers under or at poverty pay. For women, the direction of the gap changed, with a higher proportion of younger workers under the threshold. While women did bad jobs at a much higher rate than men during the twentieth century, in 2013 younger male workers were more likely to work at or below the poverty level than older women wage earners. Most of that difference was due not to the improvement of women's wages, but to the increase in the number of young men working for low wages. Being under thirty-five is now correlated with poverty wages.

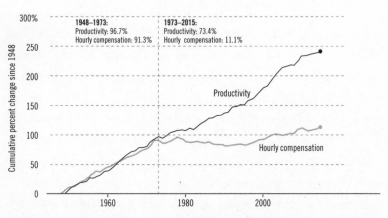

Disconnect Between Productivity and a Typical Worker's Compensation, 1948–2015

Note: Data are for average hourly compensation of production/nonsupervisory workers in the private sector and net productivity of the total economy. "Net productivity" is the growth of output of goods and services minus depreciation per hour worked.

Just because the quality of jobs has tanked, that doesn't mean the quality of workers and their work has gone down as well. Productivity hasn't followed the stagnant wage trend. In fact, nonsupervisory workers' productivity increased rapidly between 1972 and 2009, while real wages dipped.[8] Until the 1970s, both metrics grew together; their disjuncture is perhaps the single phenomenon that defines Millennials thus far. Since young workers represent both a jump in productivity and a decrease in labor costs, this means we're generating novel levels of "surplus value" — productivity beyond what workers receive in compensation. This is, of course, the goal of employers, executives, and the management consultants they hire to improve firm efficiency. It's not just their habit to step on labor costs, it's their fiduciary duty to shareholders.

3.3 Polarization

Commentators have a lot of ways to talk about the labor market's heightened stakes. A favorite one is the "skills gap," in which employers stall as they wait for better-educated workers. But that doesn't accord very well with an economy in which profits and inequality are both up.

Productive technology has aided a lot in this development, allowing managers to hyperrationalize all of their inputs, including and especially labor. The manager's job is to extract the most production from workers at the smallest cost, and managers are handsomely paid for it. Private equity firms, for example, have made untold billions by buying up companies, lowering labor costs (by means of layoffs, outsourcing, and increasing employee workloads), showing a quick turnaround in a firm's numbers, and selling it off again, all primed and ready for the twenty-first-century global economy. These corporate raiders are the market's shock troops, and over the past few decades they've twisted and prodded and cut companies into proper shape. The same forces are molding young people themselves into the shape that owners and investors want. From our bathroom breaks to our sleep schedules to our emotional availability, Millennials are growing up highly attuned to the needs of capital markets. We are encouraged to strategize and scheme to find places, times, and roles where we can be effectively put to work. Efficiency is our existential purpose, and we are a generation of finely honed tools, crafted from embryos to be lean, mean production machines.

The jobs that are set to last in the twenty-first century are the ones that are irreducibly human — the ones that robots can't do better, or faster, or cheaper, or maybe that they can't do at all. At both good and bad poles of job quality, employers need more *affective labor* from employees. Affective labor (or feeling work) engages what the Italian theorist Paolo Virno calls our "bioanthropological constants" — the innate capacities and practices that distinguish our species, like language and games and mutual understanding. A psychologist is doing affective labor, but so is a Starbucks barista. Any job it's impossible to do while sobbing probably includes some affective labor. Under the midcentury labor regime we call Fordism, workers functioned as nonmechanical parts on a mechanical assembly line, moving, manipulating, and packaging physical objects. But as owners and market pressures pushed automation and digitization, the production process replaced American rote-task workers with robots and workers overseas whenever possible — that is, whenever the firms could get ahold of the capital to make the investments.

Post-Fordism, as some thinkers call the labor model that came next, requires people to behave like the talking animals we are. Here's how Virno explains the growing demand for affective work: "In contemporary labor processes, there are thoughts and discourses which function as productive 'machines,' without having to adopt the form of a mechanical body or of an electronic valve."[9] We're still on an assembly line of sorts, but instead of connecting workers' hands, the line connects brains, mouths, and ears.

The growth of affective labor hasn't patched up the hole left by the decline in industrial labor; instead, it's driven the top and bottom of the job market further apart.

Over years of analysis, economist David Autor (of MIT and the National Bureau of Economic Research) has split work into three categories based on the type of tasks required: routine, manual, and abstract. Routine tasks characterize those middle jobs that have evaporated consistently since 1960: gigs like "bookkeeping, clerical work, and repetitive production tasks." Manual tasks, Autor writes, "require situational adaptability, visual and language recognition, and in-person interactions," and are associated with "bad" service jobs, like "janitors and cleaners, home health aides, security personnel, and motor vehicle operators."[10] Abstract tasks — tasks that involve "problem-solving capabilities, intuition, and persuasion" — have grown as a share too.[11] On both the high and low ends, more work requires the communication and understanding of emotions and ideas. This humanization of work is one of the results of firms automating mechanizable jobs in the middle of the income distribution. It also spells more work for workers; "Service with a smile" is harder than "Service with whatever face you feel like making."

What this means intergenerationally is that, as job training has become a bigger part of childhood, kids are being prepared to work with their feelings and ideas. Or, if they're on the wrong side of polarization, other people's feelings and ideas. They're being managed to work with their emotions, and to do it fast, with attention to detail, and well. Society's stressors and pressures, consciously and unconsciously, forge kids into the right applicants for the jobs of the near future.

3.4 The Feminization of Labor

The missing center of the job distribution, the routine tasks that have been largely mechanized and computerized, were built by and for male workers. As we saw earlier in the chapter, that balance has shifted, with women exceeding the male education rate and entering the workforce at higher levels and higher income brackets than they used to. This isn't just because women were cheaper and at least as competent—though that's undeniably part of it too—it's because women are better trained by society for the jobs that have been resistant to automation. British scholar Nina Power wrote about the feminization of labor in her book, *One Dimensional Woman:*

> One does not need to be an essentialist about traditionally "female" traits (for example, loquacity, caring, relationality, empathy) to think there is something notable going on here: women are encouraged to regard themselves as good communicators, the kind of person who'd be "ideal" for agency or call-center work. The professional woman needs no specific skills as she is *simply* professional, that is to say, perfect for the kind of work that deals with communication in its purest sense.[12]

On both sides of polarization, the jobs lasting and being created are "women's work," evoking the same qualities women practice every day by doing a disproportionate amount of unpaid emotional and domestic labor. Power's idea of feminization in work as a pattern within capitalist development finds support in the employment numbers. We've already seen how the gendered wage gap has narrowed in the past decades, but women not doing as badly as their counterparts hardly justifies proclaiming "the end of men," as the writer Hanna Rosin did in a monumentally popular piece for the *Atlantic* in 2010, and then in a book two years later. "Man has been the dominant sex since, well, the dawn of mankind. But for the first time in human history, that is changing—and with shocking speed,"[13] Rosin wrote. Is Millennial gender hierarchy shifting as fast as everything else?

There's decent evidence that the answer is yes, and not just at the level of theory or rhetoric. And though women's gains haven't been evenly distributed, the data on jobs confirms that we have undergone a real shift, even if it's not quite as dramatic as Rosin makes it out to be. Here's how Autor summarizes the state of American male workers since the late twentieth century:

> Males as a group have adapted comparatively poorly to the changing labor market. Male educational attainment has slowed and male labor force participation has secularly [over the long term] declined. For males without a four-year college degree, wages have stagnated or fallen over three decades. And as these males have moved out of middle-skill blue-collar jobs, they have generally moved downward in the occupational skill and earnings distribution.[14]

Combine this with the stereotype of white-collar men as less masculine than manual and routine workers, and the "feminization of labor" looks like a very real phenomenon. But instead of the optimistic portrait of female empowerment that commentators like Rosin and Sheryl Sandberg paint, feminization reflects employers' successful attempts to reduce labor costs. Women's labor market participation has grown just as job demands intensify and wages stagnate.

As we saw earlier in the chapter, the trend of women's work improving as they joined the labor force—i.e., fewer women in each generation working for poverty-level wages—has ended, and that ending coincides with the broader move toward feminization. The increase in paid work among mothers is part of an overall increase in their weekly labor hours, not a replacement for domestic tasks. It's hard to work out the exact relation, but the "end of men" definitely hasn't been a zero-sum gain for women workers, most of whom (judging by the end of progress out of poverty-level jobs) seem to have hit their heads on the glass ceiling. However, some men look at these labor market changes in the light of the expansion of women's rights within marriage (like the right to own property and decline sex) and feel they've lost ground. A smaller group of men called men's rights activists, or MRAs, have knit a total ideology around their sense of lost privilege and a desire to turn back the clock on American heterosexual relations. But their assumption that if men take a hit on the job market it's to the advantage of women is a bad guess.

The feminization of labor involves a declining quality of life for working men *and* women within heterosexual family units. In her book *Pressed for Time: The Acceleration of Life in Digital Capitalism*, sociologist Judy Wajcman explains how the process works at the family level:

> The major change has come from working women themselves, who reduce their time in unpaid labor at home as they move

into the workforce. However, they do not remotely reduce their housework hour-for-hour for time spent in paid labor. And while their male partners increase their own time in housework, this is not nearly as much as working wives reduce theirs. The upshot is that rather less unpaid household labor gets done over-all in the dual-earner household—but women's total combined time in paid and unpaid household labor is substantially greater than is the typical nonemployed women's in domestic labor alone. . . . The working woman is much busier than either her male colleague or her housewife counterpart.[15]

It's important not to blame the wrong actor and to make sure we keep our eyes on the bottom line: Women are working more overall, men are doing more housework, and yet there's less housework getting done and less financial stability. This is what happens when all work becomes more like women's work: workers working more for less pay. We can see why corporations have adapted to the idea of women in the labor force. Plus, the ownership class can redirect popular blame for lousy work relations toward feminists. Millennial gender relations have been shaped by these changes in labor dynamics, and we can't understand the phenomenon of young misogyny without understanding the workplace.

Just because some men's work tended to be better at a time when single-worker families were more common doesn't mean we can return to the former by returning to the latter. But that's the narrative misogynists use to interpret what's going on and how it could be fixed, and they've attracted a lot of angry and confused men who aren't sure about their place in the world. One antidote to this kind of thinking is an alternative framework for why and how workers (of all genders) came to be in such a precarious position.

3.5 Precarity

Like feminization, the term "precarity" has spread from radical corners to the mainstream, as commentators, analysts, and average folks alike reach for a word to describe the nature of the change in the employer-employee relationship during Millennials' lifetimes. Precarity means that jobs are less secure, based on at-will rather than fixed-duration contracts; it means unreliable hours and the breakdown between the workday and the rest of an employee's time; it means taking on the intense responsibility of "good" jobs alongside the shoddy compensation and lack of respect that come with "bad" jobs; it means workers doing more with less, and employers getting more *for* less. More than any other single term, "precarity" sums up the changed nature of American jobs over the last generation. And not only the jobs; young people curl around this changing labor structure like vines on a trellis. We are become precarity.

In his book *24/7: Late Capitalism and the Ends of Sleep,* Columbia University professor Jonathan Crary describes how market logic has forced itself into the whole of workers' daily lives. Precarity digs the basement on labor costs deeper, pushing the limits on how much employers can juice out of employees. Speaking broadly, there are three ways to do that: increase worker productivity, decrease compensation, and increase labor-time. It's the third of these that Crary focuses on in *24/7.* "By the last decades of the twentieth century and into the present, with the collapse of controlled or mitigated forms of capitalism in the United States and Europe, there has ceased to be any internal necessity for having rest and recuperation as components of economic growth and profitability," he writes. "Time for human rest and regeneration is now simply too expensive to be structurally possible within contemporary capitalism."[16] Free time can always turn to productivity, so when productivity is properly managed, there is no such thing as free time. Instead, like cell phones that are only meant to be turned off for upgrades, Millennials are on 24/7. In a Centers for Disease Control and Prevention survey, over two-thirds of high schoolers report getting fewer than eight hours of sleep per night,[17] a situation the agency has labeled a "public health crisis."[18]

Aside from the myriad physiological effects of prolonged sleep loss, this 24/7 life has serious psychosocial effects for the people who attempt it. Adjusting to being always on is hard work, and it's not for nothing. Employees who can labor when others sleep have an advantage, and in this market, someone is always willing to seize an advantage. In the start-up sector, where the main thing some entrepreneurs have to invest is their own work-time, every hour of sleep is a liability. Whether it's because of enthusiasm, economic insecurity, or too many screens with too many feeds that never stop scrolling, Millennials are restless creatures. "24/7 is shaped around individual goals of competitiveness, advancement, acquisitiveness, personal security, and comfort at the expense of others," Crary writes. "The future is so close at hand that it is imaginable only by its continuity with the striving for individual gain or survival in the shallowest of presents."[19] If enough of us start living this way, then staying up late isn't just about pursuing an advantage, it's about not being made vulnerable. Like animals that don't want to be prey, young workers have become quite adept at staying aware and responsive at all times.

This hyperalert lifestyle doesn't sound particularly appealing for the people living it, but for employers, it's a dream come true. Or, I should say, a plan come to fruition. Twenty-four/seven work is a crucial aspect of precarious labor relationships. On the unfortunate side of polarization, lower-skill jobs may not provide employees (if they're even categorized that way, rather than as "independent contractors"—or even worse, paid off the books with no official status to speak of) with a full forty-hour workweek, but that doesn't mean they're exempt from 24/7 time pressures. Employers value flexibility, and the more time workers could be *potentially* working, the more available they are on nights and weekends, the more valuable they are. You don't get paid for the time you spend available and unused, since the compensation is hourly, but part-time retail workers (for example) still can't draw a clear line between work-time and the rest of their lives, because they never know when the boss might need them. According to the National Longitudinal Study of Youth data, nearly 40 percent of early-career workers receive their work schedules a week or less in advance.[20] That's not a lot of time in which to plan your life.

On the professional side of polarization, the proportion of men and women working more than fifty hours a week has grown significantly.[21] Innovations in productive technology make it possible for these high-skill employees to be effectively at work wherever or whenever they happen to be in space and time. There have always been people who spend all their time working—some of them better compensated than others—but at least in professional jobs, this condition has generalized. No longer are a good education and a good career dependable precursors to a life with lots of leisure time. For young people who are working hard to put themselves on the successful side, they're setting themselves up for more of the same. This road is no mountain climb: It's a treadmill.

3.6 Nice Work If You Can Get It

Not only is the forty-hour workweek a thing of the past for most employees, more is required of workers during their hours. Higher productivity can sometimes sound easy, as if we were Jetson-like technolords, masters of our working domain, effortlessly commanding the robot servants that titter at our beckon. That's not how it works. As we've seen, the benefits of technological innovation haven't been well distributed. Instead, workers become more like the hyperconnected, superfast, always-on tools we use every day. And it's hard to keep up with a smartphone.

Commentators and analysts who sympathize with the employer point of view, or who believe growth to be uncomplicatedly beneficial for society, are excited by gains in hourly productivity. Kalleberg gives us another way of looking at "productivity" (the term itself betrays an employer's perspective), paying attention to the role of coercion:

> To take advantage of this potential for productivity growth, however, workers must be persuaded (or coerced) to devote high levels of effort.... Highly educated professionals and managers and those in full-time and traditional work situations have seen their hours increase and have had to work harder. Meanwhile, workers at lower-wage strata often have to put together two or more jobs to make a decent living.[22]

This is what young people are training so hard to prepare for: a working life that asks them once again to bear the costs while passing the profits up the ladder. Whether they end up on the winning or losing side of income polarization, young workers need to be prepared to work hard and often. The grand irony is that this system wouldn't be possible without a generation of young Americans who are willing to take the costs of training upon themselves. If young people refused to pay in time, effort, and debt for our own job preparation, employers would be forced to shell out a portion of their profits to train workers in the particular skills the companies require. Instead, a competitive childhood environment that encourages each kid to "be all they can be" and "reach their potential" undermines the possibility of solidarity. As long as there's an advantage to be had, Millennials have been taught to reach for it, because if they don't, someone else out there will. This kind of thinking produces some real high achievers, but it also puts a generation of workers in a very bad bargaining position. If we're built top-to-bottom to struggle against each other for the smallest of edges, to cooperate not in our collective interest but in the interests of a small class of employers—and we are—then we're hardly equipped to protect ourselves from larger systemic abuses. In a way, we invite them, or at least pave the road.

This is how the individual pursuit of achievement and excellence—the excellence and achievement that every private, public, and domestic authority urges children toward—makes Millennials into workers who are too efficient for our own good. As it happened to Danny Dunn, the predictable consequence of increasing your ability to do work is *more work*. That's what intensification is, and it's a bummer.

So far I've looked at labor trends as they've changed the entire job market, but now I want to focus on how workers experience these shifts on different ends of polarization, as well as some labor relations that don't fit simply in either category. Although precarity and intensification are common to both higher- and lower-income workers, that doesn't mean I can draw any hasty equivalences. Even if good and bad jobs are both worse than they have been in important and similar ways, as we'll see, the divisions between them—and between the lifestyles they enable—have deepened.

To get at the comparative intensity of unemployment and underemployment, we can look at other historical measures. One way the Federal Reserve Economic Data (FRED) database tracks the *quality* of unemployment is the median duration—that is, the median length of time that workers spend looking for work. From the 1970s to 2000, this measure varied cyclically between four and ten weeks, only edging above ten for seven months in the early 1980s. After the 2001 recession, the rate increased to ten before falling to eight. The 2008 recession had a more dramatic effect: In June 2010, the median length of unemployment peaked at twenty-five weeks. Since then, it has declined from this postrecession high, but the new normal (ten weeks) is off the charts compared to the twentieth century.[23] And because unemployment doesn't include so-called marginally attached workers who haven't looked for work in the four weeks preceding the survey, we can't be sure how many people have fallen off the statistical edge.

If Kalleberg is right and these changes are lasting instead of cyclical, then the twenty-first-century recessions represent a quantum jump in the nature of job-seeking. Electronic résumé and application tools like Craigslist and LinkedIn make it easier to apply, but they also make it easier for employers to dip into reserve pools of increasingly skilled labor. This follows a familiar pattern: If we're getting better and more efficient at looking for jobs, that's a good indication that we're going to be doing a lot more of it. Like work, unemployment has intensified.

When people do find a job—if they're lucky enough to do so—it's less likely than ever to be full-time. In the wake of the 2008 crisis, the number of Americans working part-time jobs for specifically economic reasons doubled, to over nine million. Since then the number has adjusted downward, but five years after the peak, only half the postrecession increase had receded.[24] This accords with what millions of Americans already know, and what we've just seen above: The lower end of job polarization is increasingly managed according to employers' whims and immediate profit concerns. The popularity of part-time jobs makes it easier for owners to efficiently toggle their labor inputs, but being toggled along with the market makes life hard for workers who can't rely on future income — never mind the predictable promotions and salary bumps that come with progress in a firm's internal labor market — or nonwage benefits like health care, pensions, severance, or sick leave.

When given the choice, employers would rather pay only for the labor-time they need, rather than assuming long-term commitments to flesh-and-blood workers who might get pregnant or fall down or get sick or need to grieve a family member or maybe just become redundant or too expensive. It's much cheaper to think of labor as a flow that can be spliced into hourly pieces to fit employer specifications, a production input like plastic or electricity, and just as subject to rationalization. (This is, of course, how accounting as a discipline and managerialism as an ideology view workers.) Having pushed so many of the training costs onto young people and their families, employers have less invested in individual employees and their continued welfare. If they didn't invest in the workers' human capital, firms aren't compelled to "protect" their investments. Management of all but the most rarefied, highest-skill workers is no longer about carrots and sticks; employers can let generalized debt and the cost of living take care of the incentives. It's a buyer's market when it comes to labor, and they get to set the terms.

3.7 Deunionization

Employers didn't just awake one day and decide to treat their workers worse. Capitalism encourages owners to reduce their labor costs until it becomes unprofitable. The minimum wage exists to put an extra-market basement on how low the purchasers of labor can drive the price. As Chris Rock famously put it: "Do you know what it means when someone pays you minimum wage? I would pay you less, but it's against the law." But the minimum wage hasn't been the strongest bulwark against the drive to depress compensation—and not just because it has lost a quarter of its inflation-adjusted value against the Consumer Price Index since the late 1960s.[25] Industrial labor unions have always attempted to counter employer interests by representing large numbers of workers together. This collective bargaining meant wages, benefits, hours, working conditions, promotions, etc., were all subject to negotiation between two parties that needed each other. If unions care about their members, and firms are compelled to care about what their unions want, then as long as their mutual dependence lasts, unionized workers can maintain some balance of power. But in the last few decades, that bit of shared leverage has largely dissolved.

According to a 2013 report from the Bureau of Labor Statistics, union membership was nearly halved since the bureau began measuring in 1983. Over the three decades, the rate dropped from 20.1 percent to 11.3 percent.[26] Everything in this chapter so far has to be understood in the context of massive deunionization in America. Although union membership rates have dropped for men and women over the past thirty years, they've fallen over three times faster for men

(12.8 vs. 4.1 percent).[27] The narrowing of this gap between the number of unionized men and unionized women is another component of the feminization of labor and the reduction of costs. Without collective bargaining, only the most in-demand employees have any leverage at all when it comes to determining the conditions of and compensation for their work.

There are a lot of proximate causes for deunionization: Automation displaced routine jobs, which are particularly suited for collective bargaining, since labor's role in production is clear and individual workers' contributions are easily compared. Because median union pay is over 20 percent higher than pay for nonunion workers, multinational firms have offshored unionized manufacturing, chasing cheaper labor from right across the border in Mexico all the way to China.[28] Republicans have tried schemes at the local, state, and national levels to undermine unions for ideological and economic reasons, but also because organized labor is a power base for Democrats. Unions themselves have been forced into a defensive position, fighting for institutional survival instead of expansion. There's also a cultural aspect: Kids trained from infancy to excel and compete to their fullest potential under all circumstances are ill-suited for traditional union tactics that sometimes require intentionally inefficient work, like the slowdown strike or work-to-rule. Instead, we're perfect scabs, properly prepared to seize any opportunity we can.

No tendency better describes the collapse of American organized labor than the decline in strike activity. In the 1970s, there were hundreds of strikes every year with thousands of workers, but by the turn of the century, the decline in membership and antistrike legislation caused the number of actions and rate of participation to drop 95 percent each.[29] A strike is how organized labor flexes its muscles; the threat that organization poses is a halt to production. Without the promise of work stoppage, union power dissipates and workers can't possibly negotiate from a position of strength.

Muscles atrophy, and solidarity can't be relied upon if young workers don't learn and practice it. At last count, a negligible 4.2 percent of workers under twenty-four belonged to unions, less than one-third the rate of workers over fifty-five.[30] The older you are (up until retirement age), the greater the chances you belong to a union, which indicates that current membership rates are soft and will decline fast as older laborers retire and die. It's not just a question of access; the BLS reports that young workers are the least likely to join and pay dues when they're hired at a unionized workplace.[31] As Millennials enter the labor force, they have been structurally, legally, emotionally, culturally, and intellectually dissuaded from organizing in their own collective interest as workers. And the plan has been successful. With the number of unemployed and part-time workers, there's no macroeconomic indication that large unions are going to regain their prominence. It looks more likely that American industrial labor unions as we've known them won't survive another generation.

3.8 Just Get an Intern

Union workers symbolize the aspects of employment that are on the decline: Members tend to be male, full-time, higher-paid, and older. They embody an American social contract and a way of life that's dying. So what is the inverse? What is the figure that represents the type of labor that's on the rise? The unpaid intern is a relatively new kind of employee. This role combines features of low- and high-skill labor, along with the lack of compensation that befits work under the pedagogical mask. Unpaid interns are more likely to be young women and work flexible hours. Most of all, they're unpaid. They do manual tasks like fetching coffee and making copies, as well as abstract tasks like managing social media accounts and contributing to team meetings. Interns have one leg in each side of labor polarization.

The intern category recently applied only in extraordinarily high-skill professions like medicine, where doctors train in a live workplace setting (and get paid a beginner wage from the government). In this traditional mode, newcomers are learning the ropes via trial and error, and if hospitals didn't need a next generation of doctors, they wouldn't be worth the trouble. The new interns, however, are more like entry-level employees whom firms have convinced most of us they don't have to pay. Although these things are hard to measure reliably, the survey data we have suggests that half of college graduates complete an internship before they're done.[32] That's a huge workforce; the most credible conservative numbers say that between one and two million interns offer their labor to firms every year.[33] Free workers undermine the demand for entry-level workers across the board; why pay for anything if you don't have to?

In his book *Intern Nation,* Ross Perlin details the explosive growth of internships, which he incisively calls "a new and distinctive form, located at the nexus of transformations in higher education and the workplace." In his analysis of the rhetoric surrounding want ads for unpaid internships, Perlin writes that the burden of getting value out of an internship has fallen to the interns themselves. Internships are no longer by and large a means of professional reproduction; rather, they have become an easy way for employers to take a free dip in the flexible labor pool. Instead of an investment in the future, unpaid internships are extractive. As we've moved into a parody world where there exists such a thing as a barista internship, the idea that young and inexperienced workers are still entitled to pay has gone out of fashion. In a job market where a letter of recommendation and a line on a résumé seem so valuable, we Millennials have shown ourselves willing to trade the only things we've got on hand: our time, skills, and energy.

Universities have done more than their share to promote unpaid internships, with some even requiring students to complete one to graduate. Many schools offer credit for internships, treating them as if they had the educational value of a course. What this three-party relationship means is that students are paying their colleges and working for companies (or the state or nonprofits), and in return both will confirm for anyone who asks that the student indeed paid for the credits and performed the labor. Interns are like Danny Dunn, getting paid in homework stickers.

From a student's perspective, an internship for credit, even if unpaid, is a simultaneous step toward both graduation and a job in her chosen field. At least, that's what students have been sold — because there's not much evidence that unpaid internships lead to favorable job outcomes. A 2013 survey by the National Association of Colleges and Employers (NACE) — an organization that exists in part to promote internships — found that graduates who had completed an unpaid internship were less than 2 percent more likely to get a job offer than the control group (37 and 35.2 percent, respectively), and their median starting salary was actually lower ($35,721 versus $37,087).[34] Considering those numbers, the whole sector looks like a confidence game in which young workers take the boss's word for it that they're not supposed to be paid yet, but if they try hard it will all work out for the best. It's a myth that unpaid internships are a crucial step to career advancement, but as far as colleges and employers are concerned, it's a very useful one.

Another legend surrounding unpaid internships is that the young people who do these not-quite-jobs are pampered, living on sizable grants from their parents. In popular culture, interns are the best dressed in the office, biding time while their future among the elite works itself into place. A survey by Intern Bridge — the other main research organization besides NACE that focuses on the internship market — found that lower-income students were more likely to take unpaid internships, whereas their higher-income peers were more likely to be found in the paid positions.[35] Also, women were significantly more likely to take unpaid internships both compared to paid work and compared to men. The myth of the rich intern has more to do with who gets to make movies and TV shows about young people than the actual young people who do this work, but it also serves a valuable purpose in the maintenance of the status quo: If firms and society in general assume that interns are being taken care of by a nonmarket agent like their family or school, they need not trouble themselves with how their interns are getting by week to week. This further entrenches the idea among young workers that they're not in a position from which to negotiate and that all they can do is work harder and try to ingratiate themselves with their bosses.

It's a sign of devastated expectations and rampant misinformation that entry-level workers believe they only have the leverage to ask the powers that be to *confirm* their labor for the record (rather than negotiating for wages). Only a generation raised on a diet of gold stars could think that way. Virtually no employer would be willing to bring in nonemployees who lose them money, which is what they want the Department of Labor to believe they're doing. Not in this economy, surely. As the Intern Bridge report says, "In point of fact, it is nonsensical to suggest that interns do not provide benefits to a company."[36] But that hasn't stopped influential college presidents from trying to prolong the internship windfall for as long as possible. In 2010, after the Department of Labor sent a reminder that internships had to abide by existing employment regulations, thirteen university presidents cosigned a letter to then secretary Hilda Solis requesting that federal authorities keep their hands off.[37]

My fear is that the prominence of the unpaid internship isn't the result of a regulatory oversight. Rather, this new labor regime is a natural and unavoidable outcome of a culture in which children are taught that the main objective while they're young is to become the best job applicant they can be. Even if federal regulators came down hard on firms for minimum-wage violations, even if they pursued a massive fraud case against universities that used federal funds to pay for potentially illegal internship programs, I believe there would remain young people willing and eager to break the rules in order to sell themselves short.

As long as American childhood is a high-stakes merit-badge contest, there will be kids who will do whatever they must to fill out their résumé. Like Tom Sawyer talking his friends into paying him *and* doing his chore, employers and colleges have convinced young people that work itself is a privilege of which they are probably unworthy. In fact, they say our contributions are literally worthless. As Perlin writes, "The power of offering something for free—that it breaks down barriers to entry, reaches a much wider audience, and evades formal structures such as budgets—is counterbalanced by a host of negative psychological baggage.... In a society hooked on cost-benefit analyses, *free* is not part of the accounting; *free* isn't taken seriously."[38] This belief spurs some short-term profitability, but it teaches people to be servile, anxious, and afraid. And those are not the type of people who get paid the kind of money that lasts.

3.9 Owners and Profiteers

A good way to read the cumulative effects of all these trends is to look at shifts in the accumulation of wealth by age. Income is a useful but incomplete metric for assessing how people are doing economically. As we noted earlier, income measures traditionally exclude money from government transfer programs, inherited wealth, and profits from capital gains, all of which influence people's lived experience. Net worth, like a balance sheet, measures the difference between a household's liquid or saleable assets and its liabilities. This metric gives us a good idea where the proceeds from increased productivity have found their home.

Of course, older households are going to have comparatively more time to stack up assets and pay down debts, so a straight-up comparison between older and younger workers doesn't tell us much. But by looking at the historical trends, we can see structural changes to the economy over the time in question start to manifest. In 2013, a group of researchers from the Urban Institute compared changes in average net worth by age between 1983 and 2010 as reported in the Survey of Consumer Finances.[39] What they found was startling: Older households have grown their wealth significantly over the time in question, while younger households have seen much smaller or even negative gains. Households at the most aged level (seventy-four and over) increased their wealth by nearly 150 percent in this twenty-seven-year period, and those between fifty-six and sixty-four saw a 120 percent gain. Other older households (forty-seven to fifty-five and sixty-five to seventy-three) had 76 and 79 percent increases, respectively. Below forty-seven, the surges start to dwindle. Households headed by Americans between the ages of thirty-eight and forty-six saw a 26 percent jump, while those twenty-nine to thirty-seven endured a 21 percent *decrease*. For those in their twenties, there was a modest boost of 5 percent. This marks a meaningful change in the progression of American generations: "As a society gets wealthier, children are typically richer than their parents, and each generation is typically wealthier than the previous one," the researchers write. "But younger Americans' wealth is no longer outpacing their parents'."[40]

Change in Average Household Net Worth by Age Group, 1983–2010

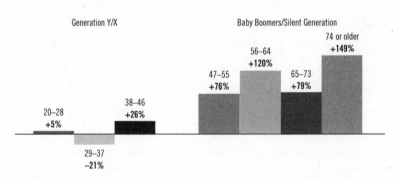

Americans have taken for granted that ours is a society getting wealthier and that children will out-earn their parents, and that has been a fair assumption. Economists use the term "absolute income mobility" to describe the relation of one generation's earning to another's, and a group at the National Bureau of Economic Research (NBER) compared the scores for Americans born in 1940 and 1980, to check on the mobility of mobility. It's no wonder we're used to feeling like things are going to get better: In the 1940 cohort, approximately 90 percent out-earned their parents. But for Millennials, the mobility number is down to 50 percent: It's a coin-flip whether or not we'll out-earn Mom and Dad.[41] The analysts conclude that the drastic change comes from the shifting, increasingly unequal distribution of GDP, rather than a lack of growth itself. The American dream isn't fading (as the title of the NBER paper says), it's being hoarded.

Still, when it comes to wealth, comparatively gradual income shifts have mattered less than the dramatic changes in debt and housing prices. Mortgage debt tends to peak when borrowers are in their late thirties, and these are the households who got caught without a seat when the subprime music stopped. Since the crisis, however, American consumers have slowed down their use of credit, deciding of their own volition to deleverage themselves. Research economists Yuliya Demyanyk and Matthew Koepke at the Cleveland Fed studied a number of trends to see if the decline in consumer credit was due to banks' unwillingness to lend or consumers' unwillingness to borrow. After assessing the credit statistics, Demyanyk and Koepke determined that the decline was more due to consumers tightening their belts than to banks tightening lending standards.[42] For the first time this century, the average consumer owns fewer than two bank cards. Although this is probably heartening to frugal-minded commentators, it also means more people are living with less.

The exception to de-escalating debt, as we've seen, is in education. Student debt has grown completely unconnected to other forms of borrowing and people's ability to pay. In 2014, Richard Fry of Pew Research Center looked at the same 2010 survey data as the Urban Institute study, specifically at households under forty and their education and student debt loads. What he found runs counter to the conventional wisdom about the value of a college degree.[43] Fry split the households under forty twice: those with a bachelor's degree ("college educated") and those with outstanding student debt. The big division comes not between either of the two splits, but between one quadrant and the other three. College-educated households without student debt had a median net worth just shy of $65,000, far higher than the three other categories combined, and over seven times greater than the $8,700 median wealth for college-educated households with debt. The average wealth for households without a bachelor's and without student debt is actually higher than that for the indebted graduates, at just under $11,000. The worst off are those without a bachelor's but who have still racked up some debt—not uncommon considering the many Americans who enter programs but don't finish, and the number in two-year and vocational programs. The wealth that's supposed to come with educational debt hasn't accrued to the tail end of Gen X yet, and it's going to get worse.

Young Student Debtors Lag Behind in Wealth Accumulation

Median net worth of young households

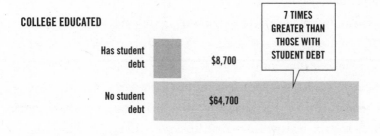

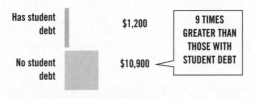

Note: Young households are households with heads younger than 40. Households are characterized based on the educational attainment of the household head. "College educated" refers to those with a bachelor's degree or more. Student debtor households have outstanding student loan balances or student loans in deferment. Net worth is the value of the household assets minus household debts.

And yet, despite all the economic instability in this young century, despite all the popped bubbles and chastened speculators, if you don't examine the distribution, things look great in America. In March of 2014, the *Wall Street Journal* was able to report the headline "U.S. Household Net Worth Hits Record High" without, strictly speaking, lying.[44] Increases in the value of stocks, bonds, and homes have driven the recovery from the 2008 crisis, even though the recovery has been unevenly enjoyed. The net acquisition of financial assets nearly tripled between 2009 and the second quarter of 2014, from $666.7 billion to $1.935 trillion.[45] Rental income has grown almost as fast, from $333.7 billion to $636.4 billion.[46] Meanwhile, employee compensation has grown 9.5 percent between 2008 and 2013,[47] only a fraction of the 50 percent swell in corporate profits between 2009 and the second quarter of 2014.[48] Postcrisis America has been a great place to own things and a really bad place not to.

What we see in the wealth numbers is not a clean-cut case of intergenerational robbery, or at least not just that. A quadrant of young households in the Pew data are doing quite well for themselves. Over the past generation, the economy has bent heavily in the owners' direction, like a pinball machine on tilt. The uneven impact of the 2008 crisis could have led to reevaluation of these trends. But it didn't. Instead, the owners of land, real estate, stocks, and bonds have increased their rate of gain at the expense of everyone else. This also means that the path from worker to owner gets steeper and more treacherous, and since few Millennials are born with a stock portfolio, fewer of us will make it up the mountain than in past generations.

The increasing wealth division between American owners and workers gives some much-needed context for the central role competition plays in young people's lives. With the middle hollowed out of the job market, there's less room for people to fall short, a thinner cushion for underdeveloped ambitions and ungrasped advantages. You either become someone who's in a position to buy stock and real estate—an ownership stake in the economy—or you work for them on their terms. It's no wonder that, when asked in a Pew poll, 61 percent of Millennial women and 70 percent of men said they aspired to be a boss or top manager.[49] But the 1 percent isn't called that because most people can join. The majority of these would-be bosses are on a fool's errand.

In the face of overwhelming odds and high stakes, a sufficient number of Millennials are willing to do whatever it takes to be a winner in the twenty-first-century economy. There are many more of us willing to do the work than there is space on the victors' podium. Even at the supposed highest levels of postcollegiate achievement, the same intense pressures pit workers against each other for a few spots on top. For his book *Young Money,* journalist Kevin Roose spoke with entry-level finance workers about their jobs, which he turned into a medium-term longitudinal study of what life is like after you win college. The large financial institutions where Roose is looking recruit almost exclusively out of the Ivy League, but an undergraduate background in finance is not necessarily required. What they want is twenty-one-year-olds who have never lost at anything in their lives, and then they want them to compete against each other.

Finance is, at root, about making money by owning and selling the right things at the right times. In an economy that increasingly rewards owners, these ownership managers are among the best-compensated workers in the country. (I'll get to the techies later.) But even though the job is all about risk, Roose's investigation suggests that a thirst for adrenaline isn't what motivates the top students at the top schools to join Goldman or Bank of America. Rather, it's risk *aversion*. Roose talked to a Goldman analyst who told him about the real motivations for the recruits he sees:

> Wall Street banks had made themselves the obvious destinations for students at top-tier colleges who are confused about their careers, don't want to lock themselves into a narrow pre professional track by going to law or medical school, and are looking to put off the big decisions for two years while they figure things out. Banks, in other words, have become extremely skilled at appealing to the anxieties of overachieving young people and inserting themselves as the solution to those worries.[50]

Once you're inside, the finance industry manages their domestic human capital the same way they treat human capital on the market. (Roose notes that Goldman Sachs renamed its human resources department Human Capital Management.)[51] First-year financial analysts are expected to explicitly renounce any other commitments and be on call at all times. Many of the well-publicized perks of working in finance — from the gyms to free food to late-night transportation — exist to encourage employees to work longer hours. After taking into account his obscene workweek, one J.P. Morgan analyst Roose interviewed calculated his post-tax pay at $16 an hour[52] — more than $5 less than the 1968 minimum wage adjusted for productivity growth.[53] This yields what Roose describes as "disillusionment, depression, and feelings of worthlessness that were deeper and more foundational than simple work frustrations."[54]

None of this is to say anyone should feel sorry for financiers — even junior ones — but it's worth understanding what is really at the end of the road for Millennials who do everything right. The best the job market has to offer is a slice of the profits from driving down labor costs. One of Roose's subjects found himself working on a deal he believed to be about rehabbing a firm, only to discover that his bosses were more interested in firing workers and auctioning equipment before selling the now "more efficient" company for a quick $50 million profit. Although they're the natural outcomes of the wage relation, work intensification and downsizing don't just happen by themselves. The profits have to be made, and the best of the best Millennials end up doing the analytical drudge work that makes superefficient production possible, then crying to reporters over their beers. It hardly seems worth it.

There is, eventually, a hard limit when it comes to extracting labor from workers. In 2013, a twenty-one-year-old summer intern at Merrill Lynch's London branch named Moritz Erhardt died after working until six in the morning three nights in a row.[55] (This isn't particularly uncommon—Roose describes the "banker's 9-to-5" as 9 a.m. until 5 a.m. the next day.) Eventually, if you work someone harder and harder without any regard for how they get themselves from one day to the next, they will quit or die. Like golden retrievers who don't know how to stop chasing a ball, Millennials are so well trained to excel and follow directions that many of us don't know how to separate our own interests from a boss's or a company's.

Chapter Four

The Feds

FUCK THE STATE I WANT MY BROTHER BACK ❦
—Katie Got Bandz

In one popular narrative, the changes I've examined so far in this book have occurred because conservatives have successfully waged a war on the welfare state. Antitax fanatic Grover Norquist summed up this plan with the eloquent and oft-repeated 2001 quote "I don't want to abolish government. I simply want to reduce it to the size where I can drag it into the bathroom and drown it in the bathtub."[1] Liberals and other Democrats believe that far-right conservatives and other Republicans have succeeded in shrinking the New Deal state, and they're well on their way to finishing the infanticide. At the same time, conservatives widely believe that liberals (particularly former president Obama himself) are out to exercise unprecedented control over American lives, from local bureaucrats all the way up to shadowy federal agencies like the NSA. What the evidence suggests is the worst of all possible scenarios: On this question, both sides are largely correct. The role of the United States government in its citizens' lives has changed significantly over the past couple of decades, and this change has had a large impact on the development of young Americans.

As a percentage of gross domestic product, the Congressional Budget Office says that neither government outlays nor revenue has changed that much since the 1970s.[2] Outlays have stayed at around one-fifth of GDP and revenues a few points below, yielding a deficit except for a couple of years around the turn of the millennium when the two switched places and we rode an irrationally exuberant economy to a small annual surplus. But spending only tells us about the dollars in and out: It doesn't tell us anything about the *composition* of that spending, it doesn't tell us where the money is actually going and whether, even though the spending has remained relatively consistent, the character of the government that is collecting taxes and spending them has changed. Thanks to the New Deal legacy, when we think of "government work," many of us think of union jobs with solid middle-class wages, benefits, and a predictable advancement ladder. These government jobs might very well be the spending that conservatives most object to, and since 2003, the ratio of government employment to population has declined—steadily and then more rapidly in the last couple of years. Now, under 9 percent of the population works for the government (local, state, federal), a lower proportion than the lean times of Reagan rule.[3]

The state has, like all employers, benefitted from increases in productivity, and has been able to invest in technological improvements to reduce the number of employees required. And just like state universities outsourcing jobs to private firms, the federal government quickly increased the use of private contractors during the George W. Bush administration. Between 2001 and 2008, annual federal spending on contractors ballooned from the neighborhood of $200 billion to over half a trillion dollars.[4] Nearly half of this spending ($248 billion in 2010, the last year in the White House report) was dedicated to defense contractors alone.[5] When the federal government does decide to add new personnel, where they hire them says a lot about the state of state priorities: The Partnership for Public Service reports that 77.7 percent of new jobs were added by security-related agencies like Veterans Affairs, Defense, and Homeland Security.[6] What little sustaining growth there is when it comes to federal employment is in the post-9/11 security sector, both in the "homeland" and abroad wherever American soldiers—and their better-paid and better-equipped contractor brethren—roam. Providing dependable middle-class careers is a shrinking part of that state's role in the twenty-first century, and since Americans are working longer, this is disproportionately affecting young people. In 1973, over 19 percent of full-time civilian federal employees were under thirty years of age; by 2013, that number was down to 7 percent.

But just because the government isn't hiring as many young people doesn't mean it's shrinking. Statistician Nate Silver broke down total government spending (local, state, and federal) between 1972 and 2011 in an attempt to suss out exactly where growth was coming from.[7] Adjusted government spending as a portion of GDP increased 9 percent on balance over the time in question. Defense spending's contribution to the balance was negative (-1.8 percent), which speaks not so much to a demilitarized America as to the end of the Cold War and the emergence of the US as a unipolar power. Infrastructure and service only added a tenth of a percent to total spending, with the 1.1 percent increase in "Protection and Law Enforcement" nearly offset by small declines in transportation, research, and education. The big increase, Silver (and every other analyst) found, is coming in entitlement spending, which makes up over 100 percent of the growth in the time he analyzed; Medicare and Medicaid costs alone make up more than half of the 9 percent increase.[8] This problem isn't particular to the state, as private spending on health care has jumped as well, more than doubling as a percentage of GDP since the 1970s, but entitlement programs are eating up a growing part of the federal budget.[9] As Silver puts it, "We may have gone from conceiving of government as an entity that builds roads, dams and airports, provides shared services like schooling, policing and national parks, and wages wars, into the world's largest insurance broker." One of the most popular adjectives for Millennials is "entitled," but the entitlement system wasn't built for us.

4.1 Not-So-Entitled Millennials

During the last third of the twentieth century, government attempts to reduce poverty among the elderly have been incredibly successful. In 1960, a full 35 percent of Americans age sixty-five and over were living under the poverty line. Now it's under 10 percent. Researchers at the National Bureau of Economic Research credit *the entirety* of this decrease to a doubling of Social Security expenditure per capita over the time in question.[10] The elderly have gone from the poorest American age demographic to the richest, in no small part due to sizable increases in state support. The problem is, the system is based on the ratio of workers paying into the system to beneficiaries, and as the population ages, the ratio between workers and beneficiaries decreases.

In 1960, there were five workers per beneficiary, but by the time the last Baby Boomer retires, the ratio will be down to two to one.[11] (And with wages stagnant, the jobs might not even be enough to support the people who work them.) In their 2014 reports, the Social Security trustees themselves estimate that by 2020 outgo will exceed total fund income; by 2033 the reserves will be totally depleted and new tax revenue will only cover 77 percent of scheduled benefits.[12] Americans who retired in the 1980s received twice as much in benefits as they paid taxes into the system, but the ratio has been declining ever since.[13] If the feds can only pay out 77 percent, Millennials will end up paying more into the system than they get in benefits. Based on the trustees' reports, the decline in elder poverty may not be a permanent change to the national fabric; rather, it could simply refer to a sizable transfer to a particular cohort of workers born before the 1970s.

Millennials, despite mostly supporting Social Security, are not naive about how much they'll benefit as compared to their elders. A March 2014 Pew study of Millennial attitudes toward entitlements revealed that a paltry 6 percent believe they will receive the full Social Security benefits that they've been promised, and 51 percent believe they will see *no benefits at all*.[14] Think about that for a moment: The average dual-earner couple will pay over a million dollars in taxes into a system that more than half of Millennials think will leave them high and dry.[15] Whether it's generosity of spirit, utilitarian analysis, or plain old resignation, the so-called entitled generation doesn't even feel entitled to our own entitlements.

Conservatives call Social Security a Ponzi scheme—the scam, made recently famous by Bernie Madoff, in which each new round of investors pays back the last one, creating the illusion of returns. It's also called a pyramid scheme, because each new layer of investors has to be bigger, but the right wants to put the system on a secure footing with another popular scam called the stock market. They want workers to invest in their own private retirement savings accounts instead of government guarantees, hoping that higher-than-government returns will make up for the diminishing worker-beneficiary ratio.

Of course, any entitlement based on the fluctuating price of stocks isn't much of an entitlement at all, and while some retirees might get lucky picking blue chips, conservatives would remove the "safety" in "safety net," leaving the elderly who make the wrong investment decisions to live on the street and eat cat food, as the Democrat talking points go. Linking retiree benefits to the stock market would also tie the month-to-month wellbeing of one of America's votingest demographics to the health of capital markets, and nothing would better ensure another round of bailouts than the threat of America's current cohort of elderly people returning to mid-twentieth-century poverty rates. Practically speaking, to anchor social security in the stock market is to offer financiers a government guarantee. Liberals don't really have a plan at all, except to safeguard current benefit levels and the retirement age and stall for time until the fund is depleted.

The reason? Neither party can really afford to piss off America's wealthiest and most organized age demographic. The American Association of Retired Persons (AARP) claims 37 million members age fifty and over. It's a nonprofit (with a for-profit arm, of course), and one of the biggest, most influential ones in the country. The AARP's two publications have larger circulations than any other magazines in the country, and they reap over $100 million a year in advertising fees. In 2013, the association brought in over $1.4 billion[16] in operating revenue, including $763 million in royalties from AARP-branded product and service providers.[17] The aged are a big and growing market, and AARP is a name they can trust. The AARP spends millions of dollars a year in lobbying on issues like health care, taxes, and entitlement reform, and they've been incredibly successful.[18] They pushed through and then protected one of the greatest antipoverty achievements in modern memory in Supplemental Security Income, changing the way the old and elderly live in this country. The AARP made Social Security the original third rail of American politics, and made sure politicians know not to betray their members' interests. It's a great strategy, and they've used it to make the government work for them. Kids, on the other hand, can't vote, and they don't have an AARP to join. And it shows.

4.2 The Juvenilization of Poverty

Before the late 1960s, the poverty rates for children, middle-aged adults, and seniors were all dropping along the same schedule, following the same slope down as shared living conditions improved. The elderly had the highest proportion of poor people, kids were next, and working-age adults dragged the total number down. But when children's poverty plateaued in the early 1970s, Medicare and nationalized Social Security payments kept rates falling for the elderly. In 1974, around when our story begins and a few years before the first Millennials were born, children's poverty overtook the rate for seniors. Since then, children's poverty has gone through a few cycles but has never dropped to 15 percent, where it had been earlier. Meanwhile, as we've seen, the elderly became the *least*-poor age demographic. By 2012, more than one in five American kids lived below the poverty line, and at 21.8 percent, the portion of children in poverty was more than twice as high as for those over sixty-five (who were at 9.1 percent).[19] Social scientists call this switch in fortunes between the old and young the "juvenilization of poverty."

While the elderly and their advocates have been able to protect and even grow their cash payments, poor children haven't exercised the same kind of leverage. In 1996, President Clinton ushered in welfare reform, replacing the Aid to Families with Dependent Children with the somewhat hectoring tone of Temporary Assistance for Needy Families (TANF). The condescending Personal Responsibility and

Work Opportunity Act put a lifetime cap on federal assistance at sixty months, required beneficiaries to find work, and left most of the details up to state governments—practically encouraging conservative state legislatures that are ideologically opposed to welfare to sabotage the system's operation. In most of the southern states, maximum TANF benefits amount to less than one-fifth of what it takes to live at the federal poverty line.[20] The programs that serve the elderly are built to succeed, whereas many if not most of TANF's architects would rather it not exist at all.

In 2012, the Center on Budget and Policy Priorities (CBPP) released a report for the sixteenth anniversary of TANF, assessing its effectiveness as a replacement program. Because TANF gets the same $17 billion in federal appropriations every year, the real value of this sum has declined with inflation; the AARP knows that trick, Social Security has a built-in Cost of Living Adjustment that keeps benefits' purchasing power steady over time as prices rise.[21] The rise in childhood poverty, the declining real funds, and the new law's restrictions have meant that the percentage of families with children in poverty receiving welfare benefits has plummeted. At the time of TANF's enactment, AFDC covered 68 out of every 100 families with impoverished kids—down from 82 in 1979. By 2014, it was down by more than half, to 23 percent. As the CBPP report put it, "TANF caseloads going down while poverty is going up means that a much smaller share of poor families receive cash assistance from TANF than they did prior to welfare reform."[22] Insofar as this was the intention, the Personal Responsibility and Work Opportunity Act has been successful. It's simplistic to say that an anomalously rich cohort of elderly people has been starving poor children of tax dollars. It's also not wrong.

In a 2014 report, the Stanford Center on Poverty and Inequality divided the nonelderly adult poverty data by age cohort for the period

1968 to 2012.[23] What their findings suggest is that it's not how old you are that matters, it's when you were born. The fluctuations in the poverty rate for adults age eighteen to twenty-four over the time in question look a lot more like the child than the adult rate. Now they come in at 20.4 percent—less than a point and a half below the childhood number. During the 1980s, the pattern settled: All things being equal, the younger you are, the better the chances that you're poor. Since then, the spread between different age groups has widened. In 1968, at the high point of twentieth-century Western intergenerational tension, there was no correlation between a nonelderly adult's age and their poverty rate, and all groups had rates within the small range of 8 to 12 percent. Now young adults are impoverished at nearly twice the rate of older adults (20.4 vs. 10.8 percent in the Stanford study). If you're trying to avoid being poor in America, since 1974 it has been better to be older and worse to be younger.[24]

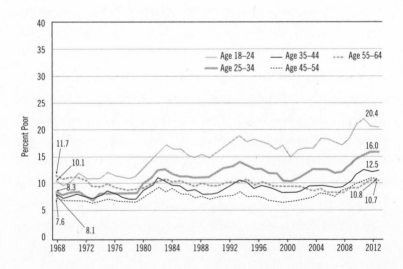

Poverty Rates for Nonelderly Adults by Age Cohort, 1968–2012

Given the state of the American social insurance system and of Millennial wealth accumulation, this age distribution trend isn't likely to hold. It seems fair to conclude that the US government did not permanently "solve" elder poverty, but instead transferred huge amounts of money to a few birth cohorts. If the Social Security trust fund runs short as predicted, then by the end of the century, the graph of the elder poverty rate over time might very well look like a deep bowl, with a low bottom for Americans born between 1915 and 1965, and sharp rises on both sides. Life-span extension could accelerate the trend, with the number of seniors increasing faster than expected as they routinely live into third and fourth decades of retirement. Government actuaries find themselves in the unenviable position of hoping people don't live too long.

These uneasy trends reemphasize that though relations between the young and the old have some immutable elements, they aren't fixed. It's a question of what kind of place you're born into, not just geographically or socioeconomically, but historically. There are lucky times and places to be born, and unlucky times and places. In America, the relatively lucky time for the average person to be born appears to be past. This is another way of putting the now widely published line that today's children and young adults are, for the first time, worse off than their parents. When history teachers talk about government policy decisions, they tend to use the progressive frame: The government improves things over time. While liberals think conservatives slow down or rewind progress, and conservatives are only willing to accept government policy forty or fifty years after its implementation (at which point they want an equal share of the credit), both agree that America is improving itself, and improving the world as it goes. This simplistic historical perspective doesn't jibe with the reality: Somehow, things got worse.

4.3 Left Behind in the Race to the Top

Education is one of the areas of public life where American policy-makers claim a lot of credit for progress. Despite all the anxiety about how US students stack up internationally, more young people are reaching higher levels of schooling, becoming more attractive potential employees. Each generation of Americans may not be better off, but they are definitely better educated. Changes at the federal level have pushed this performance inflation until it became law. Twenty-first-century primary and secondary education reform is all about efficiency and rationalized process.

In 2001, President Bush signed into law the No Child Left Behind Act (NCLB), reauthorizing what are called Title I funds (federal cash for school districts with a high percentage of impoverished students). Like welfare reform, NCLB leaves a lot up to the states, while maintaining federal standards and goals. Although it doesn't mandate *which* tests the states have to administer, participating schools have to assess their kids with a statewide standardized exam every year. The name of the law isn't quite literal, but schools were required to achieve 95 percent participation among all groups.[25] Performance inflation is written into the law as Adequate Yearly Progress, or AYP: Every year, students at any given grade level have to be testing better than the students at that grade level the year before. It's progress by declaration. According to NCLB, all students should be "proficient" or above by now.[26] Well-adjusted adults have no problem admitting there are subjects in which we underperform, but it's the official policy of the US government that all kids will be up to snuff at everything.

The penalties for not reaching your AYP goals are quick and harsh: Two years of failure means students are allowed to jump ship and head to a better school in the district, and after five the state takes over administration.[27] Many schools don't survive their sixth year of AYP failure; they're closed or turned into charters. A lot is riding on a poor school's ability to achieve the quantitative standards set up at the state and federal levels. The law is effective at incentivizing school administrations to meet their yearly progress goals, but that's not the same as incentivizing them to improve instruction or learning. Instead, it's about compelling schools to generate the right kind of data. The state accepts these assessment reports as valid representations of educational quality, so administrators and teachers—and most of all, students—have to generate the right reports.

Schools have found a lot of ways to improve their scores, demonstrating the kind of innovation that happens when the state puts a gun to your head. They've reduced arts and music time in favor of tested subjects like math and reading. Teachers spend instructional time telling kids how to fill out bubbles correctly and how to narrow choices to make a better guess. Critics call this "teaching to the test," and it's predictable and worrisome. If you threaten a school with heavy sanctions, it's no surprise that teachers will tend toward instruction geared to test performance, whether or not that's the best thing for young people's intellectual development. They will also find ways to twist the rules to their advantage by encouraging underperforming kids to drop out or stay home on testing days, or misleading high-performing students about their right to opt out of the tests. NCLB reoriented compulsory public school around the tests, and now teachers and administrators can either pour an extraordinary amount of their time and energy into complying and excelling, or they can find a new line of work.

Or they can cheat outright. The National Center for Fair & Open Testing compiled a list of more than fifty ways that schools have been caught manipulating their state testing numbers.[28] The superintendent of Atlanta's school district was indicted for racketeering after it was discovered that her nationally celebrated results were a sham: She was presiding over a giant conspiracy to defraud state and federal education authorities. From rigging testing classrooms so as to make cheating easier, all the way to teachers getting together to erase wrongs answers and fill in the right ones, schools have found and made use of work-arounds. Classrooms and teachers that look alike on paper might very well be totally different in ways the test can't see. Meanwhile, anything that's enjoyable or nurturing about school falls away if it can't be made to serve the tests.

Public school districts in areas with large low-income populations are stuck in a trap: They're being judged by the tests, as well as by graduation rates and the careers they prepare students for, but if they dedicate themselves to vocational training for middle-income jobs, of which there are fewer and fewer anyway, then whatever richer families are left will flee the district and bring down the metrics further. Scholar Nicole Nguyen found one district that's trying to thread the needle with an unconventional strategy: The whole place is focused on national security. The district in pseudonymous Fort Milton is near Washington, DC, nestled in the growing security sector. That's where the local jobs are—on both sides of wage polarization, since even the NSA's lawn care professionals need security clearances—so that's where the district put its effort. It doesn't hurt that there are lots of private and public interests happy to help, as long as there's something in it for them.

On its face, this sounds like symbiosis, or making the best of a bad situation. But some of Nguyen's observations border on the horrific. A Milton high school principal bragged about their "kindergarten-to-career pipeline," explaining that instead of counting apples, five-year-olds are counting fire trucks. "We need to catch them at that early age," he says.[29] It starts innocuously enough, but by algebra they're calculating parabolas using the trajectory of an American sniper's bullet in North Korea.[30] Military police literally patrol the hallways. Nguyen can't find much evidence that the program is actually transitioning students into national security jobs, even though "students were made to believe that they could and would secure jobs in the security industry as long as they could obtain a security clearance."[31] Regardless, military contractors have been happy to make Milton schools a showroom for edtech products, even if they're not about to hire a bunch of Milton High graduates.

The innovative thinking behind turning a school district into a private-public war academy is exactly what education reform is supposed to generate. Milton picked up a number of sizable federal grants when it switched to a security focus, which makes any district look good. Nguyen writes that "Milton's story points to how remaking public education for corporate- and military-oriented exigencies necessarily *relies on* the active role of the state, whether through funding, resources, or curriculum." But the federal government can't go in and reshape every school district, and even if they could, they wouldn't be any good at it. Instead, the feds have used an effective strategy with which we've become familiar: Put a big pile of money at the top of a hill and yell, "Race!"

Like welfare reform, contemporary education reform seems at least as devoted to tearing the past system down as to improving it. In the wake of the 2008 financial crisis, as part of the American Recovery and Reinvestment Act stimulus plan, the Obama administration put forward a $4.35-billion plan to postmodernize education. "Race to the Top" was quite literally a contest in which states competed for grants ranging from $17 million to $700 million based on school achievement and standards compliance. Trying to make over thirteen thousand districts across fifty states operate using the same curricula and testing standards is a logistical and political nightmare, so instead of trying to compel states to change the way they operate, the Obama administration let them race to rationalize. The program set up a 500-point rubric, in which states receive credit for trendy and ill-defined achievements like "using data to improve instruction" and "supporting the transition to enhanced standards and high-quality assessments."[32] It's a cost-effective way for the federal government to institute a series of reforms that it has no constitutional authority to mandate and no bureaucratic bandwidth to administer.

The most controversial of the Race to the Top provisions was forty points for adopting "common" standards.[33] The Common Core State Standards Initiative seeks to unify K-12 grade-level standards across the country, and it has met with a lot of resistance, mostly from conservatives who resent the Obama administration's overreach in meddling with the way they educate their children. But conservatives weren't the only ones upset: Some liberal and left-wing educators worry that the unified curricula are stultifying, crowd out more engaging pedagogy, and are too focused on test preparation. Both critiques were well founded; the feds defining an annual rate of progress for every child in the country from the time they enter school until adulthood *does* sound like the kind of dystopian plot a tyrannical state might undertake in an effort to create a more uniform population. And centering the academic development of American kids on math and language arts testing standards is shortsighted at best, and deeply harmful at worst.

Standardization, as we've seen in the labor market, is an important part of a rationalization process that's ultimately about lowering costs. Once we've turned educational achievement into a set of comparable returns, the policymakers and bureaucrats can focus on getting the same returns for less money. We can read this trend in the other Race to the Top scorecard items, like "improving teacher and principal effectiveness based on performance."[34] Students themselves don't have any representation, of course, even though any change in curriculum, assessments, or standards affects their lives as much as anyone's. The national education reform plan, under Republicans and Democrats, is to increase student scores. The explicit reason the increases are needed, politicians tell us, is so that kids will be ready for college and the workforce. Besides the fact that *some* children must be left behind if they're all racing to the top, job training is a lousy way to spend ages five to eighteen. Even worse if it's standardized across the whole country.

The entire way we talk about education turns students into lab rats, objects of experimentation and feedback, and Millennials were born in captivity. Stakeholders work out compromises and decide on procedures in order to create kids who will fill out the right bubbles on their standardized tests. From all the rhetoric about preparation (the Common Core calls itself "a set of clear college- and career-ready standards for kindergarten through 12th grade in English language arts/literacy and mathematics" — I wonder if these standard-makers don't feel just a *bit* silly talking about career-ready six-year-olds),[35] it's clear the American public education system is a rapidly rationalizing factory for producing human capital. They think once every school is on the same page, they can turn up output like they're producing bottle caps or bars of steel. If employers need a lot of skilled workers, then the state will provide. The workers might not be happy, but they'll know how to work. For kids who don't (or can't) fit the mold, however, getting along has become more difficult. We can draw a straight line between the standardization of children in educational reform and the expulsion, arrest, and even murder of the kids who won't adapt.

4.4 Cops

As much as policymakers wish they could erase all the differences between students except for how high their scores are, there's (thankfully) far too much variation for this to be feasible. The kind of scholastic training we have requires kids to be at least manageable if it can't make them all the same. That is, they must be instructable up to the minimum common standard, display adequate progress, and not interfere with anyone else's learning. If a kid can't manage these three things, then the school is forced to take further action. As the demand for human capital has broadened, the educational project's stakes are higher, and the higher the stakes, the lower the tolerance for disruption. The result has been schools that are disciplined and policed as if the system's goals were career preparation first and punishment second.

As we saw earlier in the section on risk elimination and zero-tolerance discipline, the modern classroom aspires to total control, to be a space where education can progress according to policymakers' predictions and employers' needs. To standardize all those students in peace, teachers and administrators have to excise the disruptive elements. School officials have accomplished this by removing more and more kids from class. A comprehensive study by Daniel J. Losen and Tia Elena Martinez of UCLA's Civil Rights Project tracked the shocking increase in suspensions at American primary and secondary schools. Comparing data from the 1972–73 and 2009–10 school years, Losen and Martinez found that the elementary school rate increased from .9 percent to 2.4 percent, while the secondary school rate increased from 8 percent to 11.3 percent.[36] That's millions of American kids who are given the scholastic equivalent of a felony conviction every year.

As if the ostensible motive for the increase in suspension—efficiency—weren't sinister enough, there's not much evidence that suspensions have a positive effect on the resulting learning environment. In a report for the Southern Poverty Law Center ("Suspended Education: Urban Middle Schools in Crisis"), Losen and coauthor Russell J. Skiba examined the studies on suspension rates and how they affect classroom ecology:

> There are no data showing that out-of-school suspension or expulsion reduce rates of disruption or improve school climate; indeed, the available data suggest that, if anything, disciplinary removal appears to have negative effects on student outcomes and the learning climate. Longitudinal studies have shown that students suspended in sixth grade are more likely to receive office referrals or suspensions by eighth grade, prompting some researchers to conclude that suspension may act more as a reinforcer than a punisher for inappropriate behavior. In the long term, school suspension has been found to be a moderate-to-strong predictor of school dropout, and may in some cases be used as a tool to "cleanse" the school of students who are perceived by school administrators as troublemakers. Other research raises doubts as to whether harsh school discipline has a deterrent value.[37]

Suspensions are a way to separate out students according to the arbitrary passions of teachers and administrators. Despite the frequent moral panics about school violence, the vast majority of suspensions are for nonviolent and often incredibly vague offenses like tardiness, disrespect, and classroom disruption. In fact, the number of in-school victimizations (like assault and robbery—crimes where people are harmed) has dropped precipitously in both absolute and relative terms (along with crime nationally) since the 1990s. The number of violent attacks was cut by more than half between the 1992 and 2011 school years, while theft declined 77.5 percent.[38] School violence is a red herring used to justify an increasingly petty and aggressive school discipline system. And as the stakes of childhood have grown, so have the consequences for kids who fall afoul of the school cops.

Like every other single trend in this story, the rise in suspension rates has not been evenly distributed. While suspensions have increased significantly for students in all demographics, there is a huge racial disparity. K-12 suspensions for white students increased from 3.1 to 4.8 percent between 1973 and 2006, while the rate for all non-white students more than doubled. Black students were suspended two and a half times as often (up from 6 to 15 percent) as in the 1970s, making them three times as likely to be removed from the classroom as whites.[39] The numbers for high schoolers are even more dramatic: Nearly a quarter of black high schoolers are suspended, a 100 percent increase over the time in question, while only 7.1 percent of white high schoolers get sent home (up from 6 percent).[40] These discrepancies start as soon as children enter schooling; a 2014 report from the Department of Education found that black students represent 18 percent of preschool enrollment but 42 percent of preschool students suspended once and 48 percent of students suspended more than once.[41]

Lately, it's not just school cops that kids have to worry about. Real officers and the criminal justice system they represent no longer stop at the schoolhouse gate. Classrooms are better policed in a metaphorical sense by teachers wielding suspensions, but also literally, by the police. For her 2011 book *Police in the Hallways,* Kathleen Nolan embedded in a New York City public high school in an attempt to learn how the new discipline was playing out in cities across the country. What she saw was closer to an authoritarian dystopia than the popular image of American high school. Nolan writes that the school felt like a police precinct or a prison, with all sorts of high-tech security apparatuses and crime-oriented discipline practices: "Handcuffs, body searches, backpack searches, standing on line to walk through metal detectors, confrontations with law enforcement, 'hallway sweeps,' and confinement in the detention room had become common experiences for students. . . . Penal management had become an overarching theme, and students had grown accustomed to daily interactions with law enforcement."[42] School administrators knew police were in charge, and police knew the same. Students did too. Teachers threatened students with prison, if not immediately, then as their inescapable future.

Bringing the police into schools to patrol the hallways and intervene in noncriminal matters, along with the increased use of suspensions, is an intensification of school discipline, analogous to the intensification of the production of human capital. The system is geared to churn out more skilled workers, but it's also meant to produce prisoners. This harsh reality lurks behind every "joke" all the teachers, counselors, and administrators tell their students about ending up in prison if they don't work hard. They can try to justify the discipline with a "tough love" philosophy, but there's no love here. The mark of "troublemaker" can be just as bad for your life outcomes as actually making trouble, especially if you're black or Latinx.

America's criminal justice system needs lives to process, and our schools are obliging by marking more kids as bad, sometimes even turning them over directly to the authorities. Nolan compares the changed atmosphere of school discipline to the changed nature of American criminal justice: "Despite critiques of the overuse of the criminal-justice system, some educators become dependent on its strategies in much the same way that neoliberal criminal-justice administrators have come to rely on low-level forms of repression, such as zero-tolerance community policing, as forms of prevention."[43] (Outside of schools this is often called "broken window" policing.) The overarching effect—if not the goal—of such low-level forms of repression at the scholastic and adult levels is to separate out black people from American civil society, and it has been getting much worse. Despite the media's efforts to get us to picture generic Millennials as white, black victims of these policies are no less "Millennial" than their white peers; in fact, insofar as they are closer to the changes in policing, they are *more* Millennial.

Once again, the progressive story about public schools making the country more equal by breaking down racial barriers to achievement does not accord with the trends and statistics. Neither does the common excuse that schools are doing their best to combat inequality in the broader society. Instead of imagining that the current state of school discipline is a malfunction in a fundamentally benevolent system, it seems more likely that one of the education system's functions is to exclude some kids. When I look at school discipline in the context of declining violence and a lack of evidence that suspensions are effective at improving students' learning conditions, I can only conclude that the actual purpose of such discipline, at a structural level, is to label and remove black kids (disproportionately) from the clearly defined road to college and career. Just as they have increased human capital production, schools have increased the production of future prisoners, channeling kids from attendance to lockdown. The school system isn't an ineffective solution to racial and economic inequality, it's an effective cause.

4.5 Pens

The liberal idea of the relation between poor children and the government is that the state has abandoned them to historical inequity, uncaring market forces, and their own tangle of pathologies. The racism isn't well veiled in this last part. Jonathan Chait, the liberal writer for *New York* magazine, gives the most concise version of this "cultural" argument for racial inequality: "It would be bizarre to imagine that centuries of slavery, followed by systematic terrorism, segregation, discrimination, a legacy wealth gap, and so on did not leave a cultural residue that itself became an impediment to success."[44]

A combination of well-tailored government programs and personal responsibility—a helping hand and a working hand to grab it—are supposed to fix the problem over time. Pathologies will attenuate, policymakers will learn to write and implement better policies, and we can all live happily ever after. The problem with the relationship between poor black and brown children and the state, liberals contend, is that it's not tight enough. Analysts speak of "underserved" communities as if the state were an absentee parent. If kids are falling behind, they need an after-school program or longer days or no more summer vacation. Unlike for the rich, who have to pay for it, for the poor, the state is a solution, not a problem. There's just one fly in the ointment: The best research says that's not really how the relationship works at all.

For his 2011 ethnography *Punished: Policing the Lives of Black and Latino Boys*, sociologist Victor M. Rios went back to the Oakland, California, neighborhood where he had grown up only a few decades earlier to talk to and learn from a few dozen young men growing up in a so-called underserved neighborhood. What he discovered was a major shift in how the law treated the young men he was working with. "The poor," Rios writes, "at least in this community, have not been abandoned by the state. Instead, the state has become deeply embedded in their everyday lives, through the auspices of punitive social control."[45] He observed police officers playing a cat-and-mouse game with these kids, reminding them that they're always at the mercy of the law enforcement apparatus, regardless of their actions. The young men are left "in constant fear of being humiliated, brutalized, or arrested."[46] *Punished* details the shift within the state's relationship with the poor, and the decline of a social welfare model (as we saw earlier in the chapter) in favor of a social control model. If the state is a parent, it's not absent; it's physically and psychologically abusive.

One of the things Rios does best in his book is talk about the way just existing as a target for the youth control complex is hard work. He calls the labor done by the young men he observed to maintain their place in society "dignity work." Earlier, I wrote that a Millennial's first job is to remain eligible for success, which involves staying sane and out of jail. Before a young person can compete to accrue human capital, they have to be part of free society. The police exist in part to keep some people at the margin of that free society, always threatening to exclude them. "Today's working-class youths encounter a radically different world than they would have encountered just a few decades ago," Rios writes. "These young people no longer 'learn to labor' but instead 'prepare for prison.'"[47] The data backs him up: A 2012 study from the American Academy of Pediatrics found that "Since the last nationally defensible estimate based on data from 1965, the cumulative prevalence of arrest for American youth (particularly in the period of late adolescence and early adulthood) has increased substantially":

> If we assume that the missing cases are at least as likely to have been arrested as the observed cases, the in-sample age-23 prevalence rate must lie between 30.2 percent and 41.4 percent. The greatest growth in the cumulative prevalence of arrest occurs during late adolescence and the period of early or emerging adulthood.[48]

Along with other kinds of youth labor, dignity work has grown. It's harder now for kids to stay clear of the law. All of the trends in school discipline (increasingly arbitrary, increasingly racist, and just plain increasing) play out the same way at the young adult level. There are many explanations for the rise of American mass incarceration — the drug war, more aggressive prosecutors, the 1990s crime boom triggering a prison boom that started growing all on its own, a tough-on-crime rhetorical arms race among politicians, the rationalization of police work — and a lot of them can be true at the same time. But whatever the reasons, the US incarceration rate has quintupled since the 1970s, and it's affecting young black men most of all and more disproportionately than ever. The white rate of imprisonment has risen in relative terms, but not as fast as the black rate, which has spiked. The ratio between black and white incarceration increased more between 1975 and 2000 than in the fifty years preceding.[49] Considering the progressive story about the arc of racial justice, this is a crushing truth.

Mass incarceration, at least as much as rationalization or technological improvement, is a defining aspect of contemporary American society. In her bestselling book *The New Jim Crow: Mass Incarceration in the Age of Colorblindness,* law professor Michelle Alexander gives a chilling description of where we are as a nation:

> The stark and sobering reality is that, for reasons largely unrelated to actual crime trends, the American penal system has emerged as a system of social control unparalleled in world history. And while the size of the system alone might suggest that it would touch the lives of most Americans, the primary targets of its control can be defined largely by race. This is an astonishing development, especially since given that as recently as the mid-1970s, the most well-respected criminologists were predicting that the prison system would soon fade away....Far from fading away, it appears that prisons are here to stay.[50]

The rise of racist mass incarceration has started to enter the national consciousness, but though the phenomenon coincides with Millennials' growth and development, most commentators don't connect the two. I insist that we must. If the change in the way we arrest and imprison people is a defining aspect of contemporary America—and I believe it more than qualifies—then it follows that the criminal justice system also defines contemporary *Americans,* especially Millennials. Far from being the carefree space cadets the media likes to depict us as, Millennials are cagey and anxious, as befits the most policed modern generation. Nuisance policing comes down hard on young people, given as they are to cavorting in front of others. Kids don't own space anywhere, so much of their socializing takes place in public. The police are increasingly unwilling to cede any space at all to kids, providing state reinforcement for zero-risk childhood. What a few decades ago might have been looked upon as normal adolescent hijinks—running around a mall, horsing around on trains, or drinking beer in a park at night—is now fuel for the cat-and-mouse police games that Victor Rios describes. It's a lethal setup.

4.6 Murderers

It's dangerous to be policed. We use the "cat-and-mouse" metaphor since it's readily at hand, but it camouflages the human stakes. Because police officers interact with Millennials more than they have with kids in the past, we're more likely to be the victims of state violence. We've already seen how that happens with harassment and arrests, but when the authorities engage young people—especially young people of color—there's another much greater risk. It's empirically the case that, a certain percentage of the time, America's armed police will murder people. It's a cost that we must consider before implementing any plan to increase law enforcement, but policymakers caught up in tough-on-crime madness overlooked it. And that's the charitable judgment; some Americans just don't care about people whom the police happen to kill.

The systematic exclusion of young black and brown Americans reaches its most visible and horrific level when the state's armed guards execute them in public, only to face the most minimal consequences, if any at all. Extrajudicial and pseudojudicial violence against racial minorities has always been a flashpoint in American society, but the qualitative change in policing over the past few decades (combined with new communications technologies) has caused this particular form of injustice to take on new resonance. A number of egregious police murders have entered the national spotlight, and though not all of them have featured young victims killed in public, many of them have.

These stories share a series of disturbing commonalities. As the police ratchet up their control of public spaces, hyperattuned to the presence of young black Americans, they put these communities in grave danger. The police, by treating their lives so casually and with such disdain, spread the message that these people aren't worth anything. No one has heeded the state's message quite like the private citizens who have taken the spirit of the law into their own hands and murdered black kids; Trayvon Martin, Renisha McBride, and Jordan Davis are some of the better-known victims. As long as state institutions keep pushing the message that these children and young adults are appropriate targets for violence and control, they're responsible for the climate they create.

State power in the twenty-first century reaches its apex in these extrajudicial murders. From the withdrawal of welfare support for the segregated schools to the lethal police flooding the street, the American government is a predator. Whether an individual Millennial is a target or not, they see all this happening to others in their cohort. So it's no surprise Millennials don't trust the state: Fewer kids are being helped by it, and more are being harmed. Solving pain and deprivation with today's government is like trying to stitch a wound with a flyswatter. The liberal solution to inequality and poverty—welfare state cooperation with individual gumption—is no solution at all, and not for the reasons conservatives moaning about welfare think. Unfounded assumptions about government benevolence have allowed the state youth control complex to mutate into this highly aggressive form. Nate Silver was only half right: America is an insurance company *and* an occupying army.

Chapter Five

Everybody Is a Star

Carly: Who gives haircuts by force?!

Sam: I don't know, but if this was a real TV show, it'd be more popular than anything on NBC.

— iCarly

From the way I've talked about Millennials so far, you might think we're robots, with no creativity to speak of. Analyzing the production of individuals based on the changing structures that influence them might be the best method we have for understanding generational change, but it also tends to downplay a lot of the best parts of being alive. Young people aren't just clay to be shaped; we also make something out of what is made of us. Kids are extremely inventive; they make songs and art and play games, and even though Millennials have less free time for this kind of activity, facility with advanced new tools allows them to create more faster. This "kids' stuff" occasionally attracts the attention of a wider audience, and a rare few young Americans become marketable stars. In this chapter, I want to look at entertainment, because it's one of the few areas where young people stand out both as amateurs and professionals. The distance between stars and the rest of us has never felt smaller, but they may hold a more rarefied place.

Unsurprisingly, the same trends that affect the quality of young people's work also affect the quality of their play. Making, recording, and distributing performances and art have never been even close to this easy, and kids are taking advantage. Between YouTube, camera-enabled smartphones, music editing software, and online platforms, most teens have everyday access to tools that were hard to imagine—never mind get your hands on—just a couple of decades ago. Everything goes magnitudes faster now, including the speed of creativity. With some talented friends and hard work, kids can now make and distribute professional-caliber media from home.

Like Advanced Placement students, aspiring stars have to work harder to stand out from an increasingly crowded field. Gone are the days of record industry stooges prowling the alleys of Seattle hunting for an authentic band willing to play ball; these are the days of rap producers throwing their beats at anyone who will listen. Hustling has always been part of trying to come up in the creative world, but like everything else, it has intensified. The Fresh Prince could rap about relaxing, but now "work" is the name of the game, from Britney Spears to Gucci Mane. Popular media production is so rationalized that there are teens who can do optimized hooks and brand strategy better than the adult professionals can.

In sports, we see the same dynamic at play as in all the other sectors we've examined: Higher rewards for stars, and increased competition for a small number of slots, have led to intensified training. Kids playing around in the sandlot has turned to preprofessional amateurism, and some amateur sports have become professional in all but their pay scale. Like any other ability, athletic skill and training are stored in the body. They're just a rarefied form of human capital, and you get them the same way: from work. Through hard practice and training, kids learn to do amazing things. Talent helps, but athletes can't get much further on talent alone than being picked first in gym class. Rationalization has turned games built on luck and fun into exemplary late-capitalist entertainment industries whose product is outstanding bodies tuned to perfection. Because sports makes human capital accumulation especially visible—we are supposed to watch, after all—it gives us special insight into the process. As capital advances, all workers become more like athletes.

5.1 Post-Soviet Training

Marv Marinovich wasn't a very good professional football player, but he understood something about the game—about the future of sports in general—that other Americans didn't. After his short NFL career, Marinovich went on to help establish strength and conditioning training as a fixture in every locker room. Compared to the Soviet Union, twentieth-century American athletic training was haphazard. (Think of *Rocky IV,* in which the USSR's champion Ivan Drago trains for a roomful of scientists measuring his punching power, while the hyper-American Rocky lugs unrefined timber around Siberia.) But Rocky's epic victory notwithstanding, the Soviet methods worked, and led them to top the medal count in seven of nine Winter Olympics and six of nine Summer Games. Marinovich studied these rationalized techniques and brought them to the NFL's Oakland Raiders. But though he was more successful as a trainer than a player, Marinovich never had the chance to make up for his failures on the field. That is, until July 4, 1969, when his son Todd was born.

Marv trained his son Todd to be a star quarterback quite literally from the time he was born. In his *Esquire* essay on the father and son Marinovich, Mike Sager describes the strict regimen:

As a baby, Todd was fed only fresh vegetables, fruits, and raw milk; when he was teething, he was given frozen kidneys to gnaw. As a child, he was allowed no junk food; Trudi sent Todd off to birthday parties with carrot sticks and carob muffins. By age three, Marv had the boy throwing with both hands, kicking with both feet, doing sit-ups and pull-ups, and lifting light hand weights. On his fourth birthday, Todd ran four miles along the ocean's edge in thirty-two minutes, an eight-minute-mile pace. Marv was with him every step of the way.[1]

Marv had thirteen specialists and advisors and consultants of all stripes donating their time to work on every part of Todd's body and game, and at the middle was Todd himself, doing the labor that other people could only advise him to do. And for a time, it worked. Marinovich was a standout high school quarterback, setting the national passing record and earning his own *Sports Illustrated* feature before he could drink. Todd told *SI* he wanted to be the best quarterback of all time, and it didn't seem farfetched.[2] With his natural talent and rationalized training, it's hard to imagine how you could possibly create a better football player than Todd Marinovich. At USC, the redshirt freshman Marinovich led the Trojans to a victory in the Rose Bowl. He made *Sports Illustrated* again, but this time he got the cover.

From there, it was all downhill. With his father's protective bubble popped, Todd began drinking and using drugs more, and behaving erratically. After a disappointing year at USC, he declared for the NFL draft, but his peak was already past. He bottomed out, moving from menial jobs to trouble with the law. Now Todd makes wood sculptures and expressionist paintings on the beach.

The Marinovich Project, as ESPN called the documentary, was a mixed success at best, but the idea that you could turn a kid into a world-class athlete stuck. And as competition for higher education slots intensified and costs rose, parents began to realize that being a star athlete entitles kids to a free ride at a top school in a way that being a star history student does not. There are no guarantees when it comes to raising kids, but practice definitely works, and one thing all athletes who play competitively share is a lot of childhood labor. The most dominant athletes are trained Marinovich-style, from toddlerhood. Tiger Woods's dad, Earl, had him putting on national television at the age of two. Venus and Serena Williams were running around a tennis court at five. Tim Lincecum—who won two Cy Young awards by the age of twenty-six—pitches using a delivery designed by his engineer dad. We use terms like "prodigy" for kids like these, but while some people are more naturally athletic than others, no one is born a champion. The way we talk about how children become athletes downplays the *work* they do. There's no question that a coach is doing labor when she tells a kid to run another lap, but once again the pedagogical mask prevents us from seeing the kids running around as working too. At a certain point they must decide to compete.

Building muscle is a great way of thinking about human capital because it's so literal: Work over time accumulates in the body. No one can do a push-up for you, and push-ups are not for sale at any price. Because this kind of human capital accumulation is physical, we can count it directly instead of looking at secondary market measures like worker productivity. In a 2013 paper for the *Journal of Strength and Conditioning Research,* a team of researchers looked at the change in body composition in American football players between 1942 and 2011. They looked at linemen and backs in particular because those are the positions at which size makes the greatest difference. What they found conforms to what we've seen about the accumulation of human capital: Football players are getting bigger and taller in general. But when the researchers look for an explanation, they cite "improved strength and conditioning programs, better overall training practices, enhanced nutritional intake, and possibly even the use of performance enhancing drugs"—but not increased work or the heightened competition that would reward it.[3] The same is true in basketball: Viraj Sanghvi analyzed NBA players by height and weight from the beginning of the league into the present. Between the 1940s, when the NBA began, and now, the average player's height jumped a substantial four inches, and the average player gained nearly fifty pounds.[4] The difference between 6'3" 175 and 6'7" 220 supports the thesis that we've witnessed a qualitative shift. American professional athletes, like other workers, are better prepared for their jobs.

Obviously, all the push-ups in the world can't make you four inches taller, so what explains this change? What it indicates is that the professional leagues are drawing on a larger pool of potential players: They've improved the process for finding, cultivating, and recruiting talent. For example, *Forbes* called the NBA's pursuit of seven-foot players "a years-long, worldwide search to identify and maximize talent unlike any other industry."[5] Globalization and rationalized recruitment have increased competition among workers in all industries, but rarely is one outstanding individual—rather than an idea, a product, or a business—worth so much to so many people.

5.2 Trophies and Moneyball

As we've seen, with money, time, and technology comes rationalization. Leading the charge in professional sports was the young Oakland A's general manager Billy Beane. Baseball has always been a game of statistics—even earning its own neologism, "sabermetrics"—but until recently the metrics weren't evolving as fast as data technology. Beane had to compete using an uncompetitive payroll, and he succeeded by relying on rigorous data analysis and bucking conventional scouting wisdom. He emphasized cutting unnecessary costs and picking up bargain players who would perform better than their contracts indicated. This so-called moneyball strategy is the same thing employers are doing in general: rationalizing to decrease labor costs. Displacing batting and earned run averages, "wins against replacement," or WAR, has become the most popular metric for player analysis. Rather than averages that middle schoolers calculate for math practice, WAR is an incredibly complex formula that tries to estimate how many team wins a particular player is responsible for. Intangibles that have mystified fans and coaches for ages no longer drive the industry, and statisticians break team sports into precise individual contributions.

Scouting has always been a romantic part of American sports. The system for recognizing talent was as disorganized and serendipitous as the distribution of talent itself, with broad networks of affiliated insiders knit together by personal relationships. Here's how Bernard Malamud described the early days of baseball scouting through the eyes of a character named Sam in his classic 1952 novel, *The Natural:*

> Tramping highways and byways, wandering everywhere bird dogging the sandlots for months without spotting so much as a fifth-rater he could telegraph about to the head scout of the Cubs, and maybe pick up a hundred bucks in the mail as a token of their appreciation, with also a word of thanks for his good bird dogging and maybe they would sometime again employ him as a scout on the regular payroll.[6]

Prospects themselves couldn't expect to be paid much more. Professional sports weren't so lucrative that most players hoped to make careers out of them, and they certainly didn't spend their childhoods eating carob in athletic academies. But as in other industries, exclusionary restrictions that protected white American workers from competition began to break down during the second half of the twentieth century. First, whites-only sports integrated, markedly improving the level of play. Then, teams figured out there was literally a whole world of potential superstars out there, almost all of whom were cheaper to sign than their domestic equivalents.

In the NBA, more than one in five players are now foreign-born. Over a quarter of MLB players were born outside the US, and cross-border financial incentives have led to the development of baseball academies throughout Latin America.[7] As the capitalists who run professional sports realize that exceptional athletic talent isn't concentrated in the English-speaking world, scouts and agents are willing to travel farther afield. The 2014 movie *Million Dollar Arm* tells the true story of sports agent JB Bernstein, who convinced investors to fund a reality show talent search in India for the best potential pitcher. In a population of a billion, he figured, there had to be at least one pro-caliber arm. He found two, signing Rinku Singh and Dinesh Patel to minor league contracts with the Pittsburgh Pirates even though neither of the javelin throwers had tossed a baseball before entering the competition. Two years after *Million Dollar Arm* came *One in a Billion,* a documentary about 7'2" Satnam Singh Bhamara, the first Indian player drafted by an NBA team. These pro sports recruiters went to India for the same reason offshoring companies do: discount labor. In an untapped market the size of India, even one in a billion is a sure bet. Globalization means more competition for American ballplayers, but it's far from the only cause.

Despite general decreases in childhood physical play, American kids are playing a lot more organized sports. In 2013, *ESPN* (the magazine) tried to examine youth sports participation—with the caveat that "Youth sports is so big that no one knows quite how big it is." The best estimates suggest that a significant majority of American kids age six to seventeen play on an organized sports team—between 20 and 30 million children every year, including a million and a half six-year-olds.[8] Title IX in 1972 forced high schools to provide equal opportunity for girls and women to participate, which has increased their participation by orders of magnitude. One survey cited by *ESPN* found that 69 percent of girls age eight to seventeen played on a school or club team the year before.

Organized sports have taken the place of self-organized play, and though league games count for their college applications in a way that sandlot ball doesn't, kids are missing out on the important experience of following and enforcing their own rules. In the age of rationalized training regimens, autonomy gets in the way of labor development. The stereotype that low-income kids disproportionately play sports as a way to escape their circumstances is wrong; instead, high parental income drives early participation. Children of low-income parents (under $35,000) join teams at a mean age of eight, while the children of high-income parents (over $100,000) start at just over six.[9] More kids planning to round out their résumés with varsity letters—or get a foot into higher education at all—means more competition at every level of amateur play. Participation trophies have become a symbol for generational weakness, but no AYSO-playing Millennial fourth grader ever owned a trophy factory—we're not giving trophies to ourselves. The market for plastic awards has grown with the level of competition, organization, and anxiety about success. And whenever we see some shiny and worthless distinction pinned to a Millennial, we should flash back to Danny Dunn and his homework prize: a low-cost reward for work that kids never realized they were doing in the first place.

Everyone has to work harder and from a younger age to have a shot at success, even if success just means starting on the middle school basketball team. One positive outcome of this trend—though perhaps not much comfort to the players working overtime—has been more entertaining amateur play, especially at the collegiate level.

5.3 Big Workers on Campus

Like the rest of higher education, college sports has become big business. Football and basketball in particular are cash cows for the schools that do well. A new college football play-off earned the NCAA (and its member universities) $470 million from ESPN in its inaugural year alone,[10] and the Association is in the middle of a fourteen-year $11-billion deal with CBS and TBS to broadcast the annual March Madness basketball tournament.[11] And that's just some of the TV money; it doesn't include apparel sales, tickets and concessions, alumni donations, or the invaluable media coverage and prestige that universities get when they win. The vast majority of teams, however, still lose money for their schools.[12]

But even if sports is not a spectacularly good investment for most schools, it's still a spectacle. College sports has become a viable replacement product for the professional leagues, and plenty of fans even prefer it. Vegas is happy to take bets, even though most of the players aren't old enough to walk into a casino. March Madness has become the most gambled-on sports event in the country, according to the American Gaming Association.[13] You might think underfunded public schools wouldn't be able to compete with big-money private universities, but there's not much difference when it comes to sports. Still, the scale of the business does mean schools are forced to wrestle for first-rate staff. The results are embarrassing: In thirty-nine states, the highest-paid public employee is a football or basketball coach. These salaries reach into the millions, buttressed by apparel endorsements and paid appearances. But even though labor compensation is astronomical when it comes to coaches and athletic directors, the NCAA has found an innovative way to keep labor costs down: It banned paying players.

Much like companies trying to get away with exploiting student labor, the NCAA invented its own category to dodge labor law. Like the intern loophole, the courts upheld "student-athlete" and exempted universities from all their responsibilities. Historian Taylor Branch examined the history of the legal term in his book-length essay *The Cartel: Inside the Rise and Imminent Fall of the NCAA.* The Association's lawyers first came up with the idea in the 1950s, in response to a death benefits claim by the widow of Ray Dennison. A scholarship player for the Fort Lewis A&M football team, Dennison died after an on-field head injury. Since he was a player for a public school's team, Dennison's widow believed she was due workers' compensation. As Branch writes, the NCAA believed otherwise:

> Did his football scholarship make the fatal collision a "work-related" accident? Was he a school employee, like his peers who worked part-time as teaching assistants and bookstore cashiers? Or was he a fluke victim of extracurricular pursuits? Given the hundreds of incapacitating injuries to college athletes each year, the answers to these questions had enormous consequences. Critically, the NCAA position was determined only by

its member institutions—the colleges and universities, plus their athletic conferences—as students themselves have never possessed NCAA representation or a vote. Practical interest turned the NCAA vigorously against Dennison, and the Supreme Court of Colorado ultimately agreed with the school's contention that he was not eligible for benefits, since the college was "not in the football business."[14]

It's a brilliant use of the pedagogical mask: Student-athletes can't be real athletes because they're students first. Everyone knows this to be a fraud, but it's easier to wink, nudge, and moralize than to contemplate the alternative: billions of dollars in labor costs. To keep the system in place, the NCAA has made a cardinal sin out of compensation. If schools are caught offering student-athletes anything above a scholarship—famously, the rules used to consider a bagel within bounds, but cream cheese a violation—the NCAA can take whatever action they please. Of course the Association isn't looking to kill any golden geese by targeting star players, but if a college athlete's future gets wrecked once in a while by a violation, that's the cost of keeping the rest in line. There's no *law* that bans paying a kid to come to your school, but the NCAA has attached the purity of amateur athletics to the idea that the players are uncompensated. What's closer to the truth is that the NCAA is fighting for survival. The minute universities start competing with each other for prospective players with cash on an open market is also the official time of death for college sports. That's why Branch calls the NCAA a cartel: Universities collude not to compete, and they all profit by keeping the labor cost low. It's a big scam, and it can't last.

What the NCAA can't admit is that they're a multibillion-dollar industry based on the unpaid labor of young athletes who have already spent years working incredibly hard just to get on the field. And just like their peers in finance, once the lucky few make it, they have earned a chance to do a whole lot more work. A 2010 NCAA survey found that—though rules state that coaches are only supposed to prevail upon their charges for twenty hours a week—student-athletes report regularly spending thirty to forty hours a week on their sports.[15] For Division I athletes, college sports is a full-time unpaid job, and a difficult one at that. In an open market, teams have to shell out sizable salaries for this kind of athletic labor, and the stars can't play by themselves; leagues need to pay for complete rosters even if the third-string catcher isn't exactly bringing in the crowds. The full amount the NCAA allows athletes doesn't approach what they're worth, no matter how fancy their school. In fact, it doesn't cover their expenses.

A study by the National College Players Association and Drexel University Department of Sport Management of the 2011–12 season looked at the top ten college basketball and football programs and found that "full-ride" student-athletes lived below the poverty line in seventeen of twenty programs.[16] Players on all twenty teams endured expenses of up to $6,904 above and beyond their scholarship. The same study estimated that if NCAA teams were forced to compete for players in cash, Division I football and basketball players would be worth $137,357 and $289,031 a year, respectively—not including endorsements and the gifts fans and boosters would no doubt shower upon student-athletes if they were allowed the chance to do so within the rules.[17] Some huge shortfalls are revealed in the study: Louisville basketball players received scholarships worth $17,370, which left them $3,730 below the poverty line. Meanwhile, the study's authors calculate a Louisville player's 2011–12 market value at over $1.6 million. Over four years, a University of Texas football player will not only miss out on $2.2 million in wages, he'll pay $14,500 above his scholarship for the privilege.[18] Coaches and schools get paid while players get worked; the system is manifestly exploitative. The only defense the NCAA can muster is that the players are students and students don't get paid.

When former UCLA power forward Ed O'Bannon filed a lawsuit against the NCAA and the video game maker Electronic Arts, he took a stand against the abuse of the student-athlete category. At the heart of the case—a class-action suit on behalf of Division I men's basketball and football players—was whether the NCAA can profit off the use of former players' likenesses without compensating them. O'Bannon can pick up a controller and play as himself in the EA college basketball game, but he had been required to permanently allow UCLA and the NCAA to license his image for free when he started playing. O'Bannon claimed a violation of the Sherman Antitrust Act: that the NCAA was unreasonably restricting trade by colluding to prevent players from licensing their likeness in a competitive environment. (EA quickly settled their part of the suit out of court for $40 million.) The NCAA claimed that schools field teams not for cash or prestige but because of their "commitment to amateurism," and these institutions would rather quit than violate the sanctity of not paying players.[19] The association argued that they couldn't be price-setting because what they're selling is education—they're "not in the football business"—and scholarship players pay close to nothing. How can they be price-setting if they don't charge anything? How can they compete any further if they've already gone all the way to zero?

In her ruling for the plaintiffs, federal judge Claudia Wilken found the NCAA unconvincing. She not only ruled that the NCAA was unreasonably restraining trade, she upended their whole conception of the athlete-school relationship. Instead of believing the story about generous schools bestowing their product on worthy amateurs for free, Wilken recognized that the relationship between universities and their players isn't one-way. She found that while many Division I football and basketball players do not pay for tuition, room, or board in a traditional sense, "they nevertheless provide their schools with something of significant value: their athletic services and the rights to use their names, images, and likenesses while they are enrolled."[20] This is a big problem for the NCAA. If student-athletes start removing the pedagogical mask and thinking of themselves as sellers of labor, they're liable to start acting like it. Judge Wilken noted that, in the absence of the NCAA "cartel," schools would undoubtedly offer the recruits for whom they compete most aggressively a share of the cash they generate.[21] Schools have engaged in anticompetitive practices in order to push the costs of competition on student-athletes and the kids who want to become them.

There's so much money in college sports that it has begun to look obscene to compensate players as little as the Association allows. The NCAA and an additional near two hundred schools funnel merchandise licensing through the Collegiate Licensing Company (CLC), which reported $4.62 billion in sales in 2012, driven by huge gains in women's apparel.[22] And despite the NCAA's shaky foundations, schools have kept adding teams. The National Football Foundation reported that the number of (highly capital-intensive) college football teams grew a steady 35 percent between 1978 and 2012.[23] The NCAA reported a record 463,000 student-athletes participating in 2012–13.[24] University business managers aren't the only ones who see what's going on. When asked about pay for student-athletes before the 2014 Final Four championship, University of Connecticut star Shabazz Napier told the assembled media, "Sometimes, there's hungry nights where I'm not able to eat, but I still gotta play up to my capabilities.... I don't see myself so much as an employee, but when you see a jersey getting sold...you want something in return." Shamed on the eve of their big night, the NCAA reversed the policy that limited student-athlete meals only a week later. As legal, political, and social attention focuses on the NCAA's mistreatment of student-athletes, the latter have begun to organize themselves to do more than win games.

The National College Players Association has existed for over a decade, but the organization gained prominence and authority as the controversy grew. During the 2013 college football season, the NCPA organized conference calls with players across the country, and, citing a number of grievances—including the threat of concussions, support for the O'Bannon case, and the need for general Association reform—players wrote "APU" ("All Players United") on their wrist tape. With the O'Bannon victory, student-athletes present and past have won more than just momentum: To pursue the case, NCAA Division I football and basketball players had to be certified as a class, a barrier many commentators feared they wouldn't be able to clear. Judge Wilken's ruling sets the stage for further litigation, including the nightmare scenario: A Fair Labor Standards Act class action on behalf of even a small number of highly profitable former college athletes for back wages could lay waste to the concept of amateurism and push the NCAA into the historical abyss.

College sports make a lot of the issues raised in this book so far more tangible. Kids compete against a growing number of their classmates for a few high-value slots. The NCAA figures that under 4 percent of high school basketball players and around 7 percent of football and baseball players will go on to college ball.[25] Years of heightened competition have increased the amount of skill and capability—we call that human capital, remember—required to make it, compelling would-be student-athletes to work longer and harder. And for the rare few who do get there, what most of them have won is a handful of years with *more* hard work that goes unrewarded. Outside baseball, with its extensive minor league system, as well as basketball and hockey with their international leagues, less than 2 percent of NCAA student-athletes will advance to the professional level. The other 98+ percent won't see a dime from sports, even though they too worked hard enough to be in the top 5 percent or so of high school players.[26] The labor that goes into star athletes doesn't just come from them or their coaches, trainers, consultants, or parents. The competition from the other 99.9 percent of players allows them to be great, but in a winner-take-all system devoted to cutting labor costs, there's more money for profiteers and the institutions that employ them if that work goes uncounted and unpaid. The pedagogical mask is an all-purpose tool for discounting young people's labor, and it's all the NCAA has left to hide behind.

5.4 Toddlers in Tiaras

The entertainment world is, at first glance, different: It's one of the few places where young people's work is recognized as work in a traditional sense. When a child actor walks on set or a teen pop star jumps in the studio, they're engaged in plain old labor, for which their employers have to pay market rate. Though custodial laws have led to some notable parent-child confrontations over who gets to control the money, from an employer's perspective, it's not necessarily any cheaper than hiring fully grown adult performers. Unlike in sports, there's no rule that restricts young entertainers from competing for wages and against adults. But this doesn't mean that young workers in the pop media industries are exempt from the structural shifts that affect their peers. Like young athletes, musicians, actors, and social media stars all give us insight into the broader changes in the lives of the rest of us nonsinging, nondancing, nonfamous young people.

One of the best analyses of how the entertainment world has changed for young artists in recent years comes from one of those artists herself: Taylor Swift. In July of 2014, Swift wrote an op-ed for the *Wall Street Journal* about shifts in how media gets made, distributed, and bought. The biggest and most dramatic difference between now and ten or fifteen years ago is digitization and the end of scarcity. Art that's reproducible has always lent itself to unauthorized copying—pirates even made bootleg copies of Shakespeare's plays—but each succeeding wave of recording and distribution technologies has made it easier. Tapes meant you could record songs off the radio, VHS meant you could record shows and movies. But everything solid melts into the cloud, and digitization means media can be copied without degrading and without limits on quantity. A file is a file is a file. Various file-sharing services—from Napster to LimeWire to Kazaa to The Pirate Bay—have made it nearly costless for nearly anyone to download or stream nearly anything. The futuristic fantasy of free access to every song, movie, game, and TV episode is more or less here.

One group that's not enjoying the total proliferation of all media is the recording industry. Swift's article quotes the Recording Industry Association of America's figures, which show the revenue from music sales declining by more than half between 2003 and 2013, from $15 to $7 billion annually. At the beginning of the new century, physical recorded media (CDs and tapes) accounted for over 95 percent of revenue; by 2013 it was down to 35 percent. In revenue for physical media, that's a decline of over $10 billion in a decade. This has meant heightened competition between professional and would-be professional artists. As Swift puts it, "It isn't as easy today as it was twenty years ago to have a multiplatinum-selling album."[27] And it isn't just unauthorized copying that has boosted competition; the same file-sharing sites host pirated recording and editing software too. It's easier than ever to create and distribute professional-caliber media: You don't even have to pay for the tools you need to create what used to be called a demo. This is the unpaid work of applying for gigs that's increasing across the board, and artists are particularly susceptible. Firms have shifted the costs of human capital development onto workers; artists are no exception. Artists can no longer wait even into their teens for a label or a studio to make them into a star, not when they're competing with peers who are willing to use whatever tools they can get their hands on to wedge themselves into the few A-list slots.

It's not just pop musicians who are fighting from childhood for the starring role. In her study of young violinists, *Producing Excellence: The Making of Virtuosos,* sociologist Izabela Wagner looks at how a field of small children playing instruments nearly as big as they are narrows to a tiny class of professional soloists. Star violinists have always started young, but the age at which they take up the instrument has decreased: In Wagner's observation group of nearly 100, 79 percent began their studies before the age of seven. The author describes the feat of becoming an international soloist who starts the violin after age eight as "nearly impossible." And even if you do start on time, that's far from a guarantee. Here's how one of Wagner's interviewees describes the odds of success: "For every ten students, one will attempt suicide, one will become mentally ill, two will become alcoholics, two will slam doors and jettison the violin out the window, three will work as violinists, and perhaps one will become a soloist."[28] Those are not good numbers, but there's always hope for that one spot. Until there's not.

Elite violinists (and other classical musicians) have always started young, but the Millennial cohort has had to compete with a different, bigger talent pool. Classical music has been popular in Japan since the 1960s, but China didn't pick it up until the late 1970s—Wagner dates it to Yehudi Menuhin's visit in 1979, which was also when talented Chinese violinists were first allowed to travel outside the country for study and competition. Until recently, the top ranks had been dominated by Eastern European émigrés and their children, particularly Jewish ones. (The violin was a way for families to escape the ghetto; stakes have been high.) But globalization has heightened the level of competition and proved there's no ethnic magic that makes for expert musicians. At the 2016 Yehudi Menuhin International Competition for Young Violinists, the top four spots in the senior competition belonged to artists from China and South Korea. Wagner's tally has only 3 percent of high-level young competitors born in the United States, and 0 percent of finalists. But that doesn't stop some families from trying.

Because of the low start age and the high level of initial investment required, violin is for intensive parents only. Accumulating a professional-sized amount of human capital by age fifteen is incredibly hard work, and pretty much no child can do it without a firm hand and constant supervision. It's a situation where multiple adults (parents, teachers, supporters) are piling their time, energy, and money directly into a single kid. It's a lot of work for everyone involved, and with the extremely long odds and long hours, it all looks like a long con. And for a lot of kids and parents, it is; one top-level teacher is open with Wagner about the practice of using money from the parents of the less talented to support the training of less wealthy, more talented students. And yet everyone keeps playing their part.

Wagner explains why parents are willing to endure the screaming and tears that come with entering the violin prodigy contest:

> According to my observations, parents in all categories tend to believe that their child's talent will enable them to prevail in the struggle that is the consequence of a saturated market. This conviction is shared by others in the direct environment of young soloists. The "aura" of a "talented child" mobilized the parents to pursue the path indicated by the teacher in the first stage of education. At that moment, and beyond, these expressions meant that their child had the potential to become a soloist.

If you dangle in front of parents the kind of 1 percent life outcome that goes with being a star, some of them will grab for it, even if objectively it's not a very good plan for their child's long-term wellbeing. Once a parent hears that their kid might have potential—as a painter, a dancer, a tennis player, a musician, whatever—all the stories of struggling artists and washed-up athletes fade to the background. At a certain point the student will have to be accountable to themselves for their own training, and that psychological discipline is one of the hardest things about making a true prodigy. Telling a child they're specially talented in a narrow way from such a young age has an impact on their self-perception, and the kids themselves have unrealistic ideas about their prospects. It's the champions and soloists everyone thinks about, not the much larger group of also-rans.

Young violinists who clear the first few big hurdles don't get to sit down and take a break. Or at least not a very long one. This is one soloist student's schedule:

Most of the week (Monday, Tuesday, Thursday, Friday) he is supervised at home:

> 8:30–9:30, French; 9:40–10:40, violin practice (scales, open strings, studies); 10:40–11:10, break; 11:10–12:10, mathematics; 12:10–1:30, lunch; 1:30–2:30, violin practice (pieces); 2:30–2:45, break; 2:45–3:30 history (or geography or natural science); 3:30–4:00, snack break; 4:00–5:00, violin (pieces, sight-reading); 5:30, dance lessons (or theory of music or choir); 7:30–9:00, dinner and free time.

Break times are laid out by the student. Free time is devoted to a short walk, book reading, dancing, and educational computer games. On Wednesday and Saturday, the student goes with a parent to take violin lessons.... Sunday is a free day, with "only" three hours of violin practice.[29]

The student in question is an eleven-year-old boy. Reading through his weekly agenda, it's obvious this is a *work* schedule. That kid is fiddling his little butt off every day, and he has to if he (and his adult teachers and assistants) want a shot at the one soloist spot. If he finds a way to skip a day, he can be sure that one of his competitors didn't. Musicality and talent are important for success, but there are a lot of other variables. A reasonable observer starts to wonder whether there's room for a therapy appointment in that schedule, or at least a damn playdate.

Most of us Millennials don't spend our childhoods training to become professional entertainers, and most of the ones who do attempt it drop out before they have to put all their eggs in a single basket. But the same patterns of work and competition that exist among elite young violinists exist at a less intense level among kids who are just hoping to get good enough jobs to live in security and peace. Everyone works, a few get paid.

There is a lot of drama in that experience, and during the Millennial lifetime an entire new category of marketing and entertainment has emerged around adolescence. Kids have even become the stars of their own workplace comedies, and a target consumer group as well.

5.5 The Birth of Tweens

In the early 1990s, *The Mickey Mouse Club*—a kids' variety show that served as Disney's minor league system—prepared and screened a string of future stars, including JC Chasez, Keri Russell, Christina Aguilera, Ryan Gosling, Britney Spears, and Justin Timberlake. With its skits, music videos, and live performances, the Club was a perfect course in pop-star training. As in college sports, stars-in-training attracted their own audiences. Chasing a wave of (highly leveraged) consumer spending, media and advertising companies set about creating the "tween" market. The demographic doesn't really refer to an age range; it refers to children with consumer choice.

In her book *Tweening the Girl: The Crystallization of the Tween Market,* Natalie Coulter dates the term's beginning to the formation of the Spice Girls in 1994.[30] Contradicting the classic idea we have about how music groups come to be, the Spice Girls were the product of a music management team who saw an opportunity to compete with popular boy bands. They placed a casting call in a trade magazine, and through rigorous competition among hundreds of young women, they picked five—making the group far more selective than Harvard or Yale. The Spice Girls were a worldwide success, drawing comparisons with the Beatles. But the Girls and their managers were better prepared to capitalize than Ringo and Co. had been, with new levels of branded merchandise and a full-length feature film (*Spice World*). Along with the success of Mouseketeer veterans, the Spice Girls represented a Marinovich moment for pop entertainment: Success could be built from the ground up.

Coulter traces the tween star lineage from the Spice Girls through the VHS star Olsen twins and Disney Channel original programming leads Hilary Duff and Miley Cyrus. Like the products of increasingly sophisticated experiments, these stars developed into better and better investments. There's of course some risk in putting so much into performers who are so young, but generally speaking, during this period the advantages of building a star from the bottom up started to outweigh the risks. This sounds cost-intensive compared to running ads against YouTube videos (it is—more on that soon), but at the time, media conglomerates were dealing with a whole new market and product line. And the tweens were a gold mine.

Disney wasn't the only company that saw an opportunity; Nickelodeon (a sub-brand of the parent company Viacom) ran ten seasons of a Millennial kids sketch comedy show called *All That* between 1994 and 2005. It was very goofy but produced a couple of enduring jokes. Original cast members Kenan Thompson and Kel Mitchell spun off a sketch about a dysfunctional fast-food joint into the movie *Good Burger,* and Nickelodeon gave the two of them their own comedy show, *Kenan & Kel.* The network followed suit with *All That* vet Amanda Bynes and her spin-off, *The Amanda Show.* Bynes went on to star in a couple of Hollywood teen flicks before transitioning to tabloid scandals full-time.

Of the thirty or so kids who performed on *All That,* most haven't had huge careers. The acting equivalent of a lucky-but-not-luckiest gig as a "working violinist" (from the Wagner book) seems to be a recurring supporting role in a TV show that lasts for a few seasons at least. Kenan Thompson has been the best long-term investment. He moved up from the minors to the majors and is (at the time of this writing) the longest-serving cast member in the history of *Saturday Night Live,* already fourteen years in at the young age of thirty-eight. But when he joined up at twenty-four, Thompson already had *eight years'* experience doing televised comedy for a national audience. His partner Mitchell didn't make the cut. Thompson was the first *SNL* player to have starred in a kids' show, but I'm willing to bet he won't be the last.

Miley Cyrus represents a real achievement for the tween industry. A signed television lead at twelve, Cyrus was a hit with *Hannah Montana* (itself about a tween star), garnering the Disney Channel its largest audience ever.[31] And she wasn't just an actress: Cyrus released her first studio album at fourteen, and if they made a plastic product, you could buy it with her face on it. Miley is one in a million, and Disney wanted to make sure they didn't miss the payout. She was the first artist to sign deals in TV, film, music, and consumer products with Disney.[32] Between her 2010 album *Can't Be Tamed* and 2013's *Bangerz,* Cyrus landed what everyone else so far had failed to: a seamless transition from tween star to teen pop sensation to mainstream A-lister. Not far behind her was Ariana Grande, star of Nickelodeon's *Sam & Cat,* whose 2013 album *Yours Truly* debuted at number one on the *Billboard* charts.[33] It appears the large media companies have concocted a formula for success so strong that they feel comfortable investing millions of dollars to develop a small number of child performers. At least, they did. Now the kids can do a lot of that investing on their own.

Just as the rationalized star machine really came into its own, the earth began to shake beneath its feet. Even though they have helped shrink the recording industry, free platforms like YouTube and

SoundCloud provide large media organizations with some obvious benefits. They filter talent and help shift the costs of developing human capital off their corporate plates. But the breakdown of the division between amateur and professional in such spaces also means the pros have to compete with the kids at home. Free platforms are changing more than just the production and distribution of content; they're having a huge effect on the form. In an August 2014 survey by *Variety,* fifteen hundred American teens were asked to rank twenty celebrities based on their favorable attributes; ten of the celebrities were the best-known Hollywood stars, according to the marketing analysis firm Q Scores, while the other half were popular YouTube personalities. The results weren't even close: YouTubers occupied the top five slots. Most people over the age of eighteen (myself very much included) would be surprised that Jennifer Lawrence was less popular than Ryan Higa, PewDiePie, and the comedy duo Smosh, and this signals a deep generational gulf in the way we consume (and produce) entertainment.[34]

5.6 YouTube and Fruity Loops

Platforms that entice users to post their own content are popular to the degree that people feel compelled to use them. The most successful digital platforms are thus the ones that are suited to the kind of content with the lowest production costs. Even though there are many emerging platforms for distributing full-length movies, it still takes a lot of time and money and people to put together a feature film. YouTube videos, on the other hand, have a production and distribution cost of virtually nothing. As a result, all sorts of new forms of short video have flooded the Internet, from makeup tutorials to "haul videos" in which shoppers empty their bags piece by piece for their web-cam. There are pimple-popping videos, nonerotic whispering videos, drug-use instructional videos, and a series where a young woman smashes bread products with her face. Every month or two a new "challenge" goes viral and people around the country perform variations on frozen tableaus or dump ice buckets on their heads or what have you. Now you can just watch the Internet instead of television, jumping from one amateur performance to the next. Younger Millennials have grown up with high-speed connections, and a whole virtual world of jokes and other content is just clicks away, an experience that is both inspiring and intimidating.

There is a lot of space for imagination, and YouTube, unlike labels and studios that have historically invested in particular performers, has little to gain from limiting the flow of new ideas and faces. Gradually, YouTube has turned itself into more than a platform, by sharing some ad revenue with its bigger stars and promoting their shows with traditional advertising. There are some YouTube millionaires, but the company only has to pay for success. The corporate risk is minimal, as the costs (to build a brand identity, foster an audience, and promote the content—all in addition to actually creating it) mostly fall to the creators themselves. It's no wonder Hollywood is having trouble keeping up: Julia Roberts just had to beat Meg Ryan; Jennifer Lawrence has to compete with every teenager in the country.

Until very recently, it was still common to talk about labels and studios foisting brands upon young and talented artists. This is the classic complaint of the grunge era: The corporate Man wants your rare talent or sound or energy, but he wants to remake your image, to sand off your edges and put you in a market-friendly package. As in other industries, the recruitment process has become a lot easier (cheaper) for employers and a lot more expensive for would-be employees. A demo with a new sound or a solid audition isn't good enough. Artists are now expected to arrive with a market-ready brand and audience, saving their corporate overlords the makeover expense. Building a brand is no longer the purview of slick besuited experts; it's the individual responsibility of every voice that wants to "make it." "The question is no longer IF you have a personal brand," Shama Hyder writes for *Forbes*, "but if you choose to guide and cultivate the brand or to let it be defined on your behalf."[35] In her article "7 Things You Can Do to Build an Awesome Personal Brand," Hyder lists tricks like "Audit your online presence," "Find ways to produce value," "Be purposeful in what you share," and "Associate with other strong brands." It's a lot of work, and it's work that firms would otherwise have to pay for, risks they would otherwise have to take. Instead, they get to cherry-pick from among a whole Internet of complete packages.

The best way for artists to make it to the next level — besides skilled brand management — is to do as much of the label's or network's or publisher's or gallery's work for them as possible. That means cultivating a fan base and producing professional-quality content, from albums to music videos to entire TV series. Platforms like YouTube and SoundCloud allow artists to upload and distribute their work for free, but they also automatically enter them in the world's largest talent-search reality contest. After all, it's where they found Justin Bieber. Why should a firm bother taking a chance on an unknown when there are relatively proven but unsigned acts littering the Internet? "In the future, artists will get record deals because they have fans — not the other way around," Taylor Swift concludes.[36] That future is already here, as Swift tells the story of a casting director choosing between two actresses based on which had more Twitter followers. Older Americans like to complain about the way many young people obsessively track our own social media metrics, but it's a complaint that's totally detached from the behavior's historical, material causes. As the *Forbes* article makes clear, personal branding shifts work onto job-seekers.

Take the case of Chief Keef. The Chicago rapper made *XXL*'s list of the hottest freshman artists in 2013 before he hit eighteen, but in today's culture industry, no one's really a rookie at eighteen. Before he made the list, Keef had already released over forty of his own songs for free online. At sixteen, he created a whole record label in waiting (what would become formalized as Glory Boyz Entertainment), to which he "signed" his friends and released their free tapes as well. Together they produced beats, wrote songs, recorded them, shot and edited videos, designed mixtape covers, and promoted their work— all without corporate oversight, assistance, or financing. By the time Interscope signed Keef, he was already a bona fide star, with the kind of brand they would have otherwise had to spend money developing. And even if they *had* bankrolled Keef's rise, Interscope would have been taking a big chance on an artist who might or might not have resonated with the public. An "unknown" is a much better bet when they've already earned themselves a million YouTube hits. Interscope got the best of all worlds: a proven hit single in "I Don't Like" (already remixed by Kanye), and a prebuilt subsidiary in Glory Boyz. But that wasn't enough: Interscope was able to put a condition on Keef's block-buster contract: If his debut album didn't sell 250,000 copies, the multialbum deal was off. The label is able to offload nearly all the risk onto the artists—in this case, a teenager and his friends. Despite the debut *Finally Rich* having hit its numbers—Keef claimed he made $100,000 per song on the twelve-track album—Interscope dropped Keef in October of 2014.

On the production side of music, technological advancement has made an even bigger difference. In the 1990s and the aughts, the biggest acts used songwriter/producers like Sweden's Max Martin, who turned pop song creation from an art into a science. Rationalized electronic production allowed producers to adapt their sound to whatever artist walked through the door, and without having to worry too much about whether the public would like it or not. But as young artists have developed an intuitive understanding of how these producers construct songs and have been able to replicate and build on it with editing and production software, they have begun to compete with the professionals on their own turf. Some of the more bubblegum of marquee acts like Katy Perry and One Direction still use songwriter/producers like Martin and his countryman Rami Yacoub, but as the laptop has become America's most popular new instrument, "DJ" has come to mean "electronic music composer," and once-marginal techno is now mainstream electronic dance music—EDM for short. Just as YouTube videos have an advantage over Hollywood films, EDM is better suited to the present moment than, say, nineties-style alt-rock. It is now much cheaper in terms of manpower, equipment, space, and difficulty to make an electronic track than to record a rock song, which means it's likely to be a more vibrant genre. That doesn't necessarily make it better, but there are more people doing it, and the form evolves more quickly as a result.

On the rap side, the disparity between the number of would-be lyricists and trained, equipped producers is decreasing. Much like their peers stuck in school or out on the practice field, the new breed of producer is, well, very productive. In 2011, the *New York Times* profiled then-twenty-year-old Lex Luger, who helped define what producers could do in this new environment. Starting in high school and armed with a laptop and a program called Fruity Loops, Luger created some of the most influential beats in contemporary rap. As he demonstrated to *Times* reporter Alex Pappademas, Luger can make one of these market-ready beats in under twenty minutes.[37] It's nearly impossible for labels to keep up with a world of amateurs all releasing music as fast as they can create it. The availability of programs like Fruity Loops opened up a whole new medium for kids. "If you didn't work in a major recording studio, you couldn't just be a kid that liked making beats, it didn't work like that," Mikey Rocks of the hip-hop duo the Cool Kids told *Fader* magazine. "Then Fruity Loops came and the Internet started cracking where you could get shit for free. Once you could download it, it was like, Let's go."[38] The means of beat production are now better distributed, and everyone who listens to music benefits. But those artists *making* the music aren't always so lucky.

For every Chief Keef or Luger, there are a hundred, a thousand kids doing similar work without hitting it big. The breakdown of what economists call "barriers to entry"—in this case, the costs of recording, editing, distributing, and promoting—means more people can make and publish more content. This is good for anyone who wants access to creative work unmediated by bigwigs in suits, but it's a boon for those suits too. Free distribution platforms level the distinctions between professional and amateur and allow the latter to pitch themselves to fans and labels. Online platforms don't compensate everyone who uploads their work, but that doesn't mean the owners can't profit. Estimates put YouTube's value at $70 billion. Even though this new production/distribution arrangement has shrunk the recording industry and allows consumers to access nearly anything they want on demand for free, it still isn't *bad* for corporations. It's just good for different corporations.

The phenomenon isn't limited to music; comedians are another group of content creators who face a similar situation. The Comedy Central series *Broad City,* for example, ran for years on YouTube before the network snatched it up. Nickelodeon's tween-defining Kids' Choice Awards now has a category for social media performers.

Kenan Thompson's level of experience was unprecedented for some-one of his age when he auditioned for *Saturday Night Live,* but nowa-days fifteen (the age at which he started acting) is late to get started making jokes online if you're hoping to go pro someday. But rap is still the best example. *Forbes* called free mixtapes "the ultimate adver-tisement," even though advertising isn't a cost that's traditionally borne by artists themselves.[39] If labels were still responsible, there's no way they could afford to pay for all these full-length promotional tapes. There's probably not a chance that networks would pay for a series or a writer to develop for years in the minor leagues and find an audience before giving them airtime. Flipping through the mixtapes on a site like DatPiff, it's hard to wrap your head around just how much work went into all of it. Hosting platforms make millions off the ads they run next to the content, and media companies save money by letting artists compete to get noticed, but the average artist ends up giving away more in exchange for less.

For this to work, artists have to be able to bear the costs. In the old story about a band becoming successful, they scrape, borrow, and steal to afford studio recording time and audio engineers so that they can transform their inspiration into some semblance of a viable prod-uct. Then, when they get their demo into the right hands, the label pays for slick design, overwrought marketing copy, collaborations with more established artists, and music videos. But with the barriers to entry falling, a band or an artist can do all of this on their own. A garage is more than a practice space; now it's a recording and design studio. And teens don't need any special training to pirate music, video, or image-editing software, and these days they can access a lot of it (or open-source versions) legitimately for free. From there, learn-ing is a question of practice and determination, qualities every aspect of Millennial life demands already. It's easier today for young people to make and distribute art, and according to the formula we've observed so far, that means they're going to shoulder a greater portion of the production costs.

The trends we've seen in this chapter affect us all as consumers and increasingly as producers. Declining labor costs change life for players from the sandlot to the majors, and for entertainers from the bedroom to the top of the charts. Because of their more visible labor, these celebs (and the amateurs who wouldn't mind joining them) offer insight into the changes that touch all Americans and shape the Millennial character. There are positives and negatives for individual creators, but in the aggregate, the trends from the labor market in general apply to these famous workers as well. Technological development leads to increased worker productivity, declining labor costs, more competition, a shift in the costs of human capital development onto individual competitors, and increased productivity all over again. Millennials are the historical embodiment of this cycle run amok, run off the rails, and we can watch the wreckage for free on YouTube after a thirty-second ad.

Chapter Six

Behavior Modification

Sissy: We're not bad people, we just come from a bad place.

—Shame *(2011)*

In economics, they measure costs in time, effort, and ultimately money. In this book, I've used the same categories to talk about how the costs of producing human capital have passed to workers over the past few decades. The Millennial character is a product of life spent investing in your own potential and being managed like a risk. Keeping track of economic costs is important, especially when so few commentators and analysts consciously consider the lives of young people in these terms. Growth and the growth of growth are what powers this system, and we've seen how that shapes Americans into the kinds of workers it needs, and what that process costs in terms of young people's time, effort, and debt capacity. But there are other kinds of costs as well. Just because economists don't consider the psychic costs for workers who have learned to keep up with contemporary capitalism, that doesn't mean we shouldn't.

More competition among young people — whether they want to be drummers, power forwards, scientists, or just not broke — means higher costs in the economic sense, but also in the area of mental health and social trust. If Americans are learning better and better to take whatever personal advantage we can get our hands on, then we'd be fools to trust each other. And as the stakes rise, we are also learning not to be fools.

In March of 2014, Pew Social Trends published the results of a survey taken between 1987 and 2012 on whether or not "generally speaking, most people can be trusted," broken down by generation.[1] The Silent Generation was able to pass most of their trust to the Baby Boomers, but Gen X took the first half of the 1990s hard, dropping all the way to 20 percent before edging up over 30 percent by the end of the survey period. But if Gen Xers are more cautious than their parents, Millennials are straight-up suspicious. Only four data points in, except for a brief Obama bump, we've hovered around 20 percent, dropping to 19 percent by 2012. The rate of American suckers born per minute shrank by half in twenty-five years.

When we think about the environmental conditions under which young Americans are developing, a lack of trust makes sense as a survival adaptation. A market that doles out success on an increasingly individual basis is not a strong foundation for high levels of social interdependence. With all youth activities centered on the production of human capital, even team sports become sole pursuits. Add this to the intensive risk aversion that characterizes contemporary parenting and the zero-tolerance risk-elimination policies that dominate the schools and the streets, and it's a wonder Millennials can muster enough trust to walk outside their own doors. The market and the institutions it influences—from the family, to the schools, to the police—select for competitiveness, which includes a canny distrust. Parents and teachers who raise kids who are too trusting are setting them up for failure in a country that will betray that trust; the black and Latinx boys in Victor Rios's *Punished* learn very quickly that they can't trust the authorities that are supposed to look out for them. Generalized trust is a privilege of the wealthy few for whom the stakes aren't so high, those who are so well-off they can feel secure even in a human-sized rat race. For everyone else, the modern American condition includes a low-level hum of understandable paranoia and anxiety. That's a cost too.

6.1 Bad Brains

There's a big difference between 40 percent of the population finding others trustworthy and 20 percent. Obviously, there's the quantity— a combination of factors cut the trust rate in half—but there's also a qualitative difference between living in the first country and living in the second. The ways we interact with each other and think about the people around us are highly mutable, and they shift with a society's material conditions. We aren't dumb, we're adaptable—but adapting to a messed-up world messes you up, whether you remain functional or not. The kind of environment that causes over 80 percent of young Americans to find most people untrustworthy is likely to have induced additional psychic maladies, and there has been no institutional safeguard to put the brakes on the market as it has begun to drive more and more people crazy.

No researcher has spent as much time examining the comparative mental health of American Millennials as psychologist Jean M. Twenge of San Diego State University, the author and coauthor of numerous papers and books on the topic. Twenge's most meaningful insights come from historical meta-analyses of results from decades of personality surveys. Her methodology is premised on the idea that the generation a person is born into has an important impact on their state of mind, at least as deep as the two traditionally recognized correlates of personality: genetics and family circumstance. Twenge describes her outlook in her 2000 paper "The Age of Anxiety? Birth Cohort Change in Anxiety and Neuroticism, 1952–1993":

Each generation effectively grows up in a different society; these societies vary in their attitudes, environmental threats, family structures, sexual norms, and in many other ways. A large number of theorists have suggested that birth cohort—as a proxy for the larger sociocultural environment—can have substantial effects on personality.[2]

In "The Age of Anxiety?" Twenge compares dozens of surveys, taken between 1952 and 1993, that asked college students and school-children to self-report their anxiety. For both groups, reported anxiety across the body of research increased linearly over the time in question. The growth was substantial—almost a full standard deviation. "The birth cohort change in anxiety is so large that by the 1980s normal child samples were scoring higher than child psychiatric patients from the 1950s," Twenge writes.[3] What Twenge and other researchers found is that temporary historical events like wars and depressions have not meaningfully affected America's long-term mental wellbeing. The Great Depression was an economic phenomenon, not a psychological one. Lasting trends, on the other hand, have really moved the needle. The sociocultural environment, for which birth cohort is a proxy, has grown increasingly anxiety-inducing. Along with a generally accepted air of mistrust, American kids and young adults endure an unprecedented level of day-to-day agitation.

Given what we know about the recent changes in the American sociocultural environment, it would be a surprise if there weren't elevated levels of anxiety among young people. Their lives center around production, competition, surveillance, and achievement in ways that were totally exceptional only a few decades ago. All this striving, all this trying to catch up and stay ahead—it simply has to have psychological consequences. The symptoms of anxiety aren't just the unforeseen and unfortunate outcome of increased productivity and decreased labor costs; they're *useful*. The Yerkes-Dodson law is a model developed by two psychologists (Robert Yerkes and John Dodson) that maps a relationship between arousal and task performance. As arousal heightens, so does performance, up to an inflection point when the arousal begins to overwhelm performance and scores decline. Our hypercompetitive society pushes children's performance up, and their common level of anxiety with it. The kind of production required from kids requires *attention*, and lots of it. The environment aggressively selects at every level for kids who can maintain an optimum level of arousal and performance without going over the metaphorical (or literal) edge. It's a risky game to play when you're wagering a generation's psychological health, and we can read the heavy costs in Twenge's results.

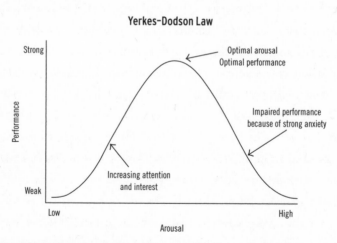

A model of the Yerkes-Dodson law at its simplest.

The dramatic psychological changes don't stop at anxiety. The Minnesota Multiphasic Personality Inventory (MMPI) is one of the oldest and most elaborate personality tests, and one of its virtues is that its endurance allows for comparisons between birth cohorts. Twenge and her coauthors analyzed MMPI results for high school and college students between 1938 and 2007. They are blunt: "Over time, American culture has increasingly shifted toward an environment in which more and more young people experience poor mental health and psychopathology," including worry, sadness, and dissatisfaction.[4] We as a society are tending toward these pathological behaviors, and for good reason.

Restlessness, dissatisfaction, and instability (which Millennials report experiencing more than generations past) are negative ways of framing the flexibility and self-direction employers increasingly demand. Overactivity is exactly what the market rewards; the finance pros whom Kevin Roose studied who *didn't* display hypomanic behavior also didn't last long on top of the world. The best emotional laborers have a sensitivity to and awareness of other people's feelings and motives that score paranoiac compared to past generations. Twenge spends a lot of energy criticizing narcissism among America's young people, but a hypercompetitive sociocultural environment sets kids up to center themselves first, second, and third. All of these psychopathologies are the result of adaptive developments.

Our society runs headlong into an obvious contradiction when it tries to turn "high-achieving" into "normal." The impossibility of the demand that people, on average, be better than average, doesn't excuse any individual child's average—or, God forbid!, subpar—performance. The gap between expectations and reality when it comes to the distribution of American life outcomes is anxiety-inducing, and it's supposed to be. Anxiety is productive, up to a limit. But increased worker precarity means most firms are less incentivized to look out for the long-term stability of their human capital assets. It's less expensive to run through workers who are at peak productivity and then drop them when they go over the edge than it is to keep employees at a psychologically sustainable level of arousal. This generation's mental health is a predictable and necessary cost of the current relations of production, a cost that is being passed to young workers.

The link between anxiety and performance is strong, but other psychological maladies are tied to intensive production even more directly. Attention deficit hyperactivity disorder (ADHD) and sluggish cognitive tempo (SCT) are both increasingly diagnosed conditions that pose a danger to children's ability to compete effectively. There's some debate within the field of psychology as to whether these constitute two separate diagnoses, but they basically refer to two different ways of being distracted in class. A kid with SCT stares out the window, while one with ADHD squirms in his seat. It's a simplification, but good enough for our limited purposes. They're attention disorders—attention being the mental work that matters more and more in (automated) American production. Students who are unable to muster the necessary attention over time can be diagnosed with an attention disorder and given medication and certain testing allowances to improve their performance. Sure, a few students are probably gaming their doctor and faking ADHD to get extra time on their SAT—but the reality is that some kids are just better at sitting still and paying attention for long periods than others, and our culture has pathologized those who aren't, because pathologies can be treated. Parents and teachers—the adults who traditionally spend the most time with children—both have good reasons to seek that treatment for low-attention kids, in order to turn them into high-attention kids. Their life outcomes might very well depend on it.

As the amount of attention required grows (more schoolwork, homework, studying, practice, etc., as in the time diaries in Chapter 1), more children will fall short. The number of American children treated for ADHD has grown significantly, from under one per hundred kids in 1987 to 3.4 in 1997[5] and from 4.8 percent in 2007 to 6.1 percent in 2011.[6] Though the two studies used slightly different age ranges, the trend is abundantly clear to all observers. Between 1987 and 1997, the socioeconomic gap in diagnosis closed as the rate for low-income kids jumped; by the turn of the century, poorer children were more likely to be labeled attention disordered.[7] In 1991, the Department of Education released a memorandum that clarified the conditions under which students with attention disorders were entitled to special education services, giving students who think they might fit the diagnostic criteria incentive to get certified by a medical professional.[8]

The most popular (on-label) medications for ADHD are stimulants like Adderall and Vyvanse, which chemically boost a user's ability to concentrate and get to work. And with millions of children and young adults taking these pills, a thriving secondary market has sprung up among people who want to increase their performance without the medical formalities. One study of nonmedical use by college students found rates of up to 25 percent, with abuse concentrated among students with lower grades at academically competitive universities.[9] The steady flow of drugs from legitimate prescriptions makes illicit use impossible to contain. Whatever the official justifications for distributing them into the environment, many young people—diagnosed and not—routinely use amphetamines to keep up in the race to accumulate human capital. It's not for nothing they call it "speed."

In the context of zero-tolerance school discipline, heavier law enforcement, and intensive parenting, increased medicalization of attention deficiency looks a lot like another form of youth control, a way to keep kids quiet, focused, and productive while adults move the goalposts down the field. Still, there's not much an individual can do about it. Once again, we're confronted with the conflict between what nearly everyone will recognize as a social problem ("Too many kids are being medicated to improve their academic performance") and the very material considerations that weigh on any particular decision ("But my kid is having a *really* hard time focusing, and the PSAT is only a year away!"). This system demands too much of children — that must be clear by now — and if a pill can help them handle it better, with less day-to-day anguish, and maybe even push them toward better life outcomes, what parent or teacher could say no? A minority, as it turns out. Of American children currently diagnosed with ADHD, more than two-thirds receive medication.[10]

There are a lot of ways to think about the widening of these diagnoses and the prescriptions used to manage them. For an individual parent, it might very well be a question of helping a child cope with an overwhelming sociocultural environment. Teachers face all sorts of pressures when it comes to the performance of their students (recall the high-stakes testing that undergirds education reform), and guiding a disruptive pupil toward medication can make their lives a lot easier. Employers want employees loaded with human capital, with a superior ability to focus and a casual relationship to the need for sleep. How they get that way isn't so much the boss's concern. Kids themselves who take a long look at the world around them might well decide to ask for some pills — and then again, they might not have much of a choice. (Some students do a different calculation and start selling the "study aids" to their classmates.) Underneath all the concerned rhetoric about young people abusing medication, there's no way to be sure that America can maintain the necessary level of production without it. And we're not likely to find out. The economy runs on attention, and unending growth means we're always in danger of running a deficit. In this environment, a pill that people believe can improve focus will never lack for buyers.

Given the psychological burden that Millennials bear compared to earlier generations, we can also expect an increase in depression. The competitive system is designed to turn everyone into potential losers; it generates low self-esteem like a refinery emits smoke. It's very difficult to imagine that the changes in the American sociocultural environment have not led to more of the population suffering from depression. Sure enough, another Twenge-coauthored meta-analysis suggests that depression has increased 1,000 percent over the past century, with around half of that growth occurring since the late 1980s.[11] If we're counting costs, then a tenfold increase in depression is a huge one, with an emotional cost to our population that's immeasurably bigger than the half-trillion dollars a year that *New York Times* reporter Catherine Rampell estimated depression costs the American economy.[12] It's another case of firms passing production costs to workers themselves, and depression has the added benefit of hiding social costs behind the veneer of individual psychosis or incapacity. But as Twenge reminds us, birth cohort is a proxy for changes in the *social* environment, and the increase in depression over time shows us that this is not a problem that emerges from the isolated turbulence of sick minds. These emotional costs are real, and Millennials bear them more than any generation of young people in memory.

6.2 Pills

Within the past few decades, the prevalence of these psychic maladies has grown fast, but not as fast as the use of medication. The refinement and popularization of selective serotonin reuptake inhibitors, or SSRIs (like Prozac), for depression, and stimulants such as methylphenidate (like Ritalin) for ADHD during the late 1980s and early-to-mid-1990s, changed the mainstream American relationship to pharmaceuticals, especially for young people. Average child brains were long considered too developmentally fragile for psychoactive medication, but by the mid-1990s even two-year-olds began popping pills. According to a 2000 article in *JAMA,* between 1991 and 1995 the number of preschoolers on antidepressants doubled, while the portion taking stimulants tripled.[13] Teens saw similar increases: Between 1994 and 2001, American teens doubled both their antidepressant and stimulant prescription rates.[14] But these numbers don't reflect an increased national willingness to deal with young people's mental distress. Over this period, the percentage of teen visits to the psychiatrist resulting in the prescription of a psychotropic drug increased ten times as much as visits overall.[15] The portion of patients undergoing psychotherapy fell by over 10 percent between 1996 and 2005.[16] In the aggregate, this looks a lot like what doctors call "drug-seeking behavior."

As we would expect based on the increased reports of psychic distress, a growing number of young people know what the inside of a psychiatrist's office looks like and how to manage their dosage. To get to this point required more than heavier academic schedules and the addition of special testing allowances for students with the right diagnoses—though both these things happened around the same time and probably helped. Pharmaceutical companies had to get the word out to people about better living through chemistry, and the population couldn't be trusted to open the Yellow Pages to "P" without prompting. Bribing doctors could only go so far. Big Pharma decided to go right to the source: In 1981, Merck printed the

first direct-to-consumer (DTC) prescription pharmaceutical adver-
tisement.

By now the "Ask your doctor" refrain is written so deep in the
American consciousness that it's hard to believe the whole category is
so young, but DTC advertising is a recent invention. In 1985, the Food
and Drug Administration claimed jurisdiction over the regulation
of DTC and applied the "fair balanced" standard—manufacturers
would have to list all potential drawbacks in medication ads, which
made radio and TV spots that satisfied the regulation so long they
were unaffordable. But over time, the FDA relaxed their position, and
in 1997 they began allowing advertisers to direct viewers to an 800
number or a website for the full list of risks.[17] DTC advertising
boomed, from $12 million in 1980 to a peak of over $5 billion by
2006. (Recall that the whole music recording industry is now worth
an annual $7 billion.)[18] Pharmaceutical companies were whispering
right in the population's ear; DTC is now "the most prominent type
of health communication that the public encounters."[19]

It's impossible to tease apart the causes of elevated psychotropic
medication among American young people: They're undeniably facing more mental pressure than their elders; they have better medications available; more attention and participation are required of them;
intensive parenting promotes frequent intervention in child development; and there's a whole new multibillion-dollar industry dedicated
to telling them they might be better off with a prescription. But
we can draw correlations between changes in the American sociocultural environment over the past few decades and the mass drugging
of children. This trend isn't a system error, it's an attempted solution
to a series of problems with young people who are alive right now.
Youth psychology became a Goldilocks question, with "just right"

lying between depression and ADHD. For everything else, there are antidepressants and stimulants—and who can blame any individual for trying to stay happy, sane, or eligible for success by any means available?

These medications don't always have the desired effects, but despite the increased levels of mental distress, the teen suicide rate has stayed just about flat, while there's been some growth in the young adult rate.[20] It's a relief that child and young adult suicide hasn't skyrocketed along with psychological health problems, but this nothing tells us something. That there hasn't been a sharp *decrease* in suicides suggests that our aggressive medication regimen is not just an instance of science providing answers or a new awareness of an old problem. If we were dealing with the same amount of depression (with more diagnoses and medication), we'd expect these higher levels of treatment to have an impact on suicide. Instead, it appears that all this medication has at best merely contained suicides at their past level, getting enough young people from one day to the next despite their greater mental duress.

Though once again there's no way to isolate cause and effect, based on the context already established, it looks like hypermedication is designed to solve new problems. It's not hard to draw the line between increased baseline adolescent mental distress, the popularization of psychoactive meds as a part of child-rearing, and higher required levels of productivity; they constitute a cluster of recent social phenomena, a constellation in the shape of a generation. If the goal has been to develop a birth cohort able to withstand the pressures of twenty-first-century production, America has succeeded. We don't have to like it, we just have to do it. When it comes to social media, however, we mostly do like it.

6.3 Social Media

When mainstream American commentators talk about the changes that have produced the Millennial psychosocial environment, they like to use a metonym: social media. "Twitter Is for Narcissists, Facebook Is for Egotists";[21] "Selfies, Facebook, and Narcissism: What's the Link?";[22] "Is Facebook Making Us Lonely?"[23] This is in part because content about social media tends to get shared on the platforms it references, making it successful and replicable according to site analytics, but the practice isn't totally off the mark. One of the major differences between Americans now and Americans thirty or forty years ago is the proportion of our interactions mediated by algorithms and scored by metrics.

As a way to rationalize interactions, social media capitalizes on and further develops young people's ability to communicate. These platforms flatten the distinctions among individuals, companies, and brands, and allow users of all sorts to measure the resonance of their every message. Social media is a good example of a lot of Millennial phenomena at the same time, but there's a danger in framing it as the source. Facebook can give us a lot of insight about young Americans, but it's only a superficial cause of behavior. Before I get into how these Internet technologies affect the Millennial character, I think it's important to look at how they affect the Millennial situation. That is, how they relate to what I've discussed in previous chapters on shifts in workforce dynamics.

From Friendster to Myspace to Facebook to Twitter, or so the social networking story goes, firms have found new ways to connect person-shaped nodes and turn those connections into large piles of investment capital and sometimes ad revenue. Users put together a personal patchwork of hardware and software, year by year getting more fluid at creating and sharing. In relation to social media, everything from photographs to videos to writing to ads becomes content. For professional and amateur creators, there's so much potential attention, and the rewards for securing a slice seem so large, that opting out of social media is like hiding away in an attic. You just can't compete that way. For this cohort of young Americans, social media is hard to separate from sociality in general, and opting out is a deviant lifestyle choice. Followers and fans used to be for cult leaders and movie stars, but social media platforms have given everyone the ability to track how much attention is being paid to each of us. Instead of just consumers, the default settings make Americans (and Millennials in particular) producers in the attention economy.

As we saw in the last chapter with YouTube and SoundCloud, social media has upsides and downsides for users at all levels. Every platform has its success stories, each producing its own handful of expert users and cross-platform stars. The best example of an app creating its own genre isn't YouTube, it's Vine. The Twitter offshoot allowed users to record six-second looping videos with sound, and some young performers amassed millions of followers, the kind of fan base that sets you up to make actual money. The top Viners formed a sort of labor cartel, promoting each other's work on their channels, talking to each other about their working conditions, and even living together. In the fall of 2015, as they saw other platforms developing more attractive deals for creators, they went to Vine with an offer:

> If Vine would pay all 18 of them $1.2 million each, roll out several product changes and open up a more direct line of communication, everyone in the room would agree to produce 12

pieces of monthly original content for the app, or three vines per week.

If Vine agreed, they could theoretically generate billions of views and boost engagement on a starving app. If they said no, all the top stars on the platform would walk.[24]

The company balked: They weren't the *boss* of these *workers,* they were a *platform* for these *creators.* The young workers withdrew en masse, some going to YouTube, others to Snapchat or Instagram. A year later, stagnated, Vine was toast. This was a rare case when creative Internet labor was organized enough and held enough leverage to negotiate collectively, but the important lesson from the story is that platforms would rather disappear entirely than start collective bargaining with talent. Which is too bad, because Vines were cool and now no one can make them—though other companies have of course replicated many of Vine's functions.

Young people's creativity is a mine for finance capital, and social media companies (usually built and maintained by young people) are the excavation tools. Precisely targeted advertisements refine the raw attention into money. From this perspective, technology firms are motivated to maximize user engagement, regardless of its impact on their lifestyle. Whether you're a beginner comedian, athlete, novelist, photographer, actor, sex worker, marketer, musician, model, jewelry maker, artist, designer, landlord, inventor, stylist, curator, filmmaker, philosopher, journalist, magician, coder, statistician, policy analyst, or video gamer, there are universally accessible and professionally legitimate platforms where you can perform, distribute, and promote your work. This may not increase the number of people who can make a living doing any of these things, or the quality of their lives. It may not mean that more or better people can see their dreams realized.

But it is a way for investors to profit off even the worst rappers and the weakest party promoters. The situation also raises the baseline hustle required for most people to succeed in any of these pursuits. At the very least you need to maintain a brand, and to do that you probably need to create social media content on someone else's platform. As a symbiotic relationship between different holders of investment capital, social media is a great low-cost way to generate, corral, measure, and monetize the attention we pay each other as we go about our affairs.

Social media seeks to integrate users of all ages, but young Americans are better suited for most platforms. With the exception of the professional résumé site LinkedIn, a 2017 Pew survey found that younger adults were more likely to use all examined social networks. That reflects a wider overall rate of Internet usage among young people: Pew only surveyed Americans over eighteen, but 99 percent of those under thirty use the Web—compared to 64 percent of seniors.[25] In an earlier report, Pew included teens. What they found is that over the past decade teens have consistently used the Internet more than other birth cohorts, and young adults have only caught up as Internet-using teens born in the late 1980s aged into the older demographic. (Although the bounds on the Millennial cohort aren't yet well defined, social media use from childhood may be what separates us from Generation Z, or whatever we end up calling the next one.)

The "digital divide" between privileged young people with computer access and underprivileged ones without seems to be closing: Pew's survey found weak or no correlation between teen computer and smartphone ownership and parental income. Among the surveyed group, 80 percent have their own computer and another 13 percent have a common computer they use at home. Of rural teens, 99 percent of the Pew group had regular online access—including 79 percent on their mobile device.[26] I expect that in the near future the statistically closable gaps in American teen Internet use will indeed close. Not everyone can access the Web, but a greater proportion of teens can log on than American adults can read a book.[27]

Just because rich and poor teens are using the Facebook app at similar rates doesn't mean they're using the same data plans. But the really successful platforms are within reach for a large majority of young Americans, so the rich kids of Instagram are an exception, not the rule. The real money is in the feelings, thoughts, ambitions, work, and *attention* of large numbers of people—preferably everyone. If only the privileged can use an app, it's a niche service with a shrinking niche. Even editorial publications like *Gawker* and *BuzzFeed* have sought to become platforms where users can create content instead of just viewing and sharing it. The platform Medium has so muddled the distinction between paid writing and unpaid blogging that even I can't tell the difference half the time. From the perspective of decreasing labor costs, it's a no-brainer: A page view earned by user-created content costs less to produce than a click on employee-created content. With a large enough user base willing to upload or publish their work for free, it's cheaper to host than to employ—even as these conditions drive down worker compensation and drive up productivity.

The Internet-enabled market tends toward this vicious, profitable cycle. A firm that can bring an aspect of social life online and speed it up—taking a Lyft, ordering takeout on GrubHub, planning an event on Facebook, finding a date on Tinder, annotating rap lyrics on Genius, recommending a restaurant on Yelp, renting an Airbnb apartment, etc.—stands to profit as a middleman, as a harvester of attention and data for advertisers, or just from demonstrated potential to do so in the future. Social media theorist Rob Horning's comments on the so-called sharing economy (where sites network and rationalize users' haves and wants, so you can rent your neighbor's chain saw, for instance, instead of buying one yourself) apply more broadly:

> The sharing economy's rise is a reflection of capitalism's need to find new profit opportunities in aspects of social life once shielded from the market, in leisure time once withdrawn from waged labor, in spaces and affective resources once withheld from becoming a kind of capital. What sharing companies and apps chiefly do is invite us to turn more of our lives into capital and more of our time into casual labor, thereby extending capitalism's reach and further entrenching the market as the most appropriate, efficient, and beneficial way to mediate interaction between individuals. For the sharing economy, market relations are the only social relations.[28]

Capitalism has always rewarded those who have found ways to monetize new life processes, but technology combined with the growth of the finance sector has accelerated this process. The Internet and social media are three-way relations among people, corporations, and technology, and they represent a major advance in the efficient organization of communication and productivity. It's clear by now that, as far as most people are concerned, in terms of the total changes in their life circumstance, this is not a fortunate thing to have happen while you're alive. Netflix is great, but it doesn't make up for labor's declining share of national production.

Proponents call the process by which investors remake activities in their own image of rationalized efficiency "disruption." The moniker lends an evolutionary sheen to the network that links every Uber and Airbnb from Silicon Valley to New York City, but disruption in this context implies a contained reorganization that follows. Tech profiteers believe the same social instability that enables their rise will settle just in time for them to get comfortable on top. It's possible they're right, but a stable "disrupted" America means further developing the tendencies we've seen in the past chapters: more polarization and inequality, declining worker compensation, increased competition, deunionization, heavier anxiety, less sleep, wider surveillance, and lots of pills and cops to keep everything manageable. This helps explain why Facebook designed and funded an entire police substation for Menlo Park, California, where the company's headquarters are located. "It's very untraditional, but I think it's the way of the future," Police Chief Bob Jonsen told the *San Francisco Examiner*.[29]

Of course, if using apps *just* made you feel isolated, broke, and anxious, fewer people would probably use them. Instead, all of these technologies promise (and often deliver) connectivity, efficiency, convenience, productivity, and joy to individual users, even though most of the realized financial gains will accrue to a small ownership class. The generalized adoption of these technologies helps bosses grow their slice of the pie, but that doesn't necessarily make using them any less irresistible for the rest of us. Coke tastes good even once you've seen what it can do to a rusty nail. Why do untrusting young Americans continue to download apps made by companies that they realize on some level are watching, tracking, and exploiting them?

Researcher danah boyd took up this question in her 2014 book *It's Complicated: The Social Lives of Networked Teens*. With a title taken from the most nuanced option in Facebook's drop-down menu for relationship status, the book contains boyd's qualitative research into the way a varied cross section of American young people uses social networking platforms. When she asked teens why they use social media, boyd heard that "they would far rather meet up in person, but the hectic and heavily scheduled nature of their day-to-day lives, their lack of physical mobility, and the fears of their parents have made such face-to-face interactions increasingly impossible."[30] Asking why teens use Facebook is a lot like asking why teens like talking to each other. "The success of social media must be understood partly in relation to this shrinking social landscape," boyd writes.[31] Driven from public spaces like parks and malls, teens have found refuge online, where their flirting, fighting, and friending can be monitored and sold to investors and advertisers.

The links between using an app and kids being forced out of public space may seem tenuous and theoretical, but once in a while we see them crystallized in an instant, as happened a few years ago in the heart of gentrifying Silicon Valley, San Francisco's Mission District. The previous home of Mexican immigrants, white flight, punk venues, and Central American refugees, the Mission has seen its character change with the influx of young tech workers. A private infrastructure has sprung up to accommodate them, spurring landlords and developers to drive the current population out with evictions and rent hikes. As part of this process, the local government contracted the management of a pickup soccer field to a group called San Francisco Pickup Soccer, a front for the national for-profit ZogSports. A "social sports league for young professionals," ZogSports organizes fee-based team play in advance — these games aren't "pickup" in any sense of the word. (Recall the discussion in Chapter 5 of the increasing organization of amateur sports.) The city contracted the field out Tuesdays and Thursdays between 7 and 9 p.m. to ZogSports in what Connie Chan, deputy policy director for the parks department, told the blog *MissionLocal* was "an experiment with new mobile app technology."[32] This tech advance in amateur sports facility management is a boon for the area's corporate activities coordinators, but not so much for the kids who want to play some soccer.

In September of 2014, a cell phone video surfaced[33] of a corporate team from Dropbox attempting to remove a bunch of local kids in time for their scheduled 7 p.m. game with Airbnb. The city's new policy conflicts with the field's own informal rules (seven-on-seven, winner stays), but the uniformed Dropbox team has their reservation in order and is unconcerned with the codes they're disrupting. In the video, you can hear a kid responding to one of the impatient players threatening to call the cops. After their game, odds are those kids headed off to do something more *productive,* whether it was homework, joining an organized sports team, or even sending a friend the link to a Dropbox full of movies. I'm willing to bet not one of those kids would trade their cell phone for another hour on the pitch — nor should they have to in order to feel legitimately aggrieved — but the totality of these technosocial changes corners children into behavior that companies can use.

The trends all stitch together — even the Dropbox employees are still with their coworkers (at least some of whom are clearly dicks) at 7 p.m. when they could be playing an actual pickup game with their friends and otherwise building social ties that aren't related to their productivity. In her book *The Boy Kings,* former Facebook employee Kate Losse described what it was like working in the early days for the company that would have such a large effect on the way so many other people would work in the near future. "Looking like you are playing, even when you are working, was a key part of the aesthetic, a way for Facebook to differentiate itself from the companies it wants to divert young employees from and a way to make everything seem, always, like a game."[34] Play is work and work is play in the world of social media, from the workers to the users.

Employees reflect on their employer's brand, and playing pickup soccer is great branding, especially if you can beat Airbnb. "Looking cool, rich, and well-liked was actually our job," Losse writes, "and that job took a lot of work."[35] Nice work if you can get it, as my mom used to say, but it's work still. Losse enjoys parts of the camaraderie, the free trips, the in-team flirting, but even the party-working takes more out of employees than it gives back. "At Facebook, to repurpose the old feminist saying, the personal was professional: You were neither expected nor allowed to leave your personal life at the door."[36] Millennials have grown up with this vision of an integrated work life as aspirational, and not because we're easily distracted by ostensibly free yogurt. (Or not *just* because.) If a Millennial does well enough to end up on the right side of job polarization, there's a good chance that their employers are willing to offer some low-cost incentives to keep them working late. Access to the office snack cabinet is an index of a worker's value in the labor market, if not of their job security. Social media means we all could be working all the time, but the people who design the platforms get perks.

The people who populate the platforms with amateur content, however, can't expect to get free yogurt, or gym memberships, or wages, even though their quality content makes the difference between a moribund site and a vibrant one. Some older adults get very excited when they start to see just how vast and diverse the ocean of user-generated content truly is. The experience can be dizzying. In their book *Born Digital: How Children Grow Up in a Digital Age,* John Palfrey and Urs Gasser are psyched to discover that kids are putting thought into their actions. "Many young users are digital 'creators' every day of their lives," they enthuse. "When they write updates in a social media environment or post selfies, they are creating something that many of their friends will see later that day.... Sometimes young people even create entirely new genres of content—such as 'memes.'...Although memes might look silly or seem irrelevant from an adult perspective, they are nevertheless creative expressions that can be seen as a form of civic participation."[37] Their tone is adorable, but also a bit quaint. The medium is not the totality of the message, a lesson I hope we all learned when Nazi frog memes played a noticeable role in the 2016 presidential election.

Networking platforms are an important part of both contemporary American profit-seeking and child development; it's like investors built water wheels on the stream of youth sociality. Through social networking interaction, kids learn the practice of what political theorist Jodi Dean calls "communicative capitalism": how to navigate the "intensive and extensive networks of enjoyment, production, and surveillance."[38] Dean writes that this education—and even attempts to resist it from the inside—ultimately serves to "enrich the few as it placates and diverts the many."[39] For all the talk about the crowd and the grassroots and the Internet age of access, for all the potentials of open source and the garage-to-mansion Internet success stories, increased inequality and exploitation have come hand in hand with these technological developments. Not only are many of young Americans' interactions filtered through algorithms engineered to maximize profits, the younger "digital native" Millennials have never known anything different. They have always been online, and their social world has always been actively mediated by corporations.

Social networking doesn't exist in a world apart; the inequalities that structure American society show up in new ways online. In *It's Complicated,* danah boyd describes how adult authorities use social networking as an investigative tool for their aggressive disciplinary apparatuses. Social media use is broadly popular, but it's still concentrated among the young and black, the same group targeted by the police and courts.[40] Intensive parenting—a practice more common among the upper classes—also encourages the strict surveillance of children's Internet use; some parents even require kids to hand over their account passwords. Whether it's by the state, their corporate hosts, or Mom and Dad, "teens assume that they are being watched," boyd concludes.[41] To adapt, young Americans have developed a host of countersurveillance techniques; boyd talked to one teen who deletes her Facebook page every day so adults can't watch her, then resurrects it at night when the observers are off the clock.[42] But even resistance like this is work that prepares young people for their future employment. Finding a way to use the Internet with a compelling personal flair but without incriminating or embarrassing yourself is an increasingly important job skill, and an even more important job-seeking skill.

6.4 Good Habits

Millennials are highly sensitized to the way our behavior is observed, both by our peers and by adult authorities. We've learned to self-monitor and watch each other, to erase, save, or create evidence depending on the situation's particular demands. Contemporary childhood prepares kids to think like the adults tracking us, and then to try to think a step further. And yet, despite all the surveillance and counter-measures, young Americans have less illicit behavior to hide in the first place. When it comes to sex, most illegal drugs, and crime, Millennials are significantly better-behaved than earlier birth cohorts. Moral panics about youth behavior are a historical constant, but now they are especially unmoored from reality.

With all the increased stress and anxiety, combined with the normalized use of prescribed pharmaceuticals, a reasonable observer might think Millennials are set up for elevated rates of substance abuse. At first glance, the numbers suggest this is the case: Lifetime illicit drug use among high schoolers is up, after a long and precipitous decline between 1980 and the early 1990s. But not all illegal drugs are created equal: When you factor out marijuana (the most popular and least harmful of controlled substances), there's a different picture: Teen drug use excepting weed has continued to decline since the 1990s, pushing historical lows.

The Monitoring the Future project at the University of Michigan's Institute for Social Research has kept detailed track of teen substance use since the beginnings of the War on Drugs in the mid-1970s. Their studies survey teens about four categories for a battery of substances: use, perceived risk, disapproval, and availability. From the late 1970s to the early 1990s, marijuana use declined, while perceived risk and disapproval increased.[43] But in the decades since, an opposing normalization trend has erased those earlier changes, putting teen pot-smoking attitudes and behavior back where they were in the mid-1970s. Since 2012, most tenth and twelfth graders no longer see "great risk" in regular use. National polling data suggests teens are ahead of the policy curve when it comes to liberalizing ideas about weed: Over four decades of national polling on marijuana legalization, Gallup's data shows a clear trend toward favoring, from merely 12 percent in 1969 to 58 percent by 2013.[44] In 2012, Colorado and Washington became the first states to legalize personal use in spite of the federal government's ongoing prohibition. In 2015, Alaska and Oregon joined them; in 2016 it was California, Nevada, Maine, and Massachusetts. If the trend continues, today's grade schoolers may have to learn from a textbook about how marijuana used to be banned.

As localities relax the restrictions on marijuana use—whether through legalization, decriminalization, or medical provisions—even getting high is getting more efficient. Handheld vaporizers are now a luxury toy for rich Baby Boomers, and years of conscious breeding means weed with a higher average psychoactive content. But smoking and vaporizing plant matter is too inefficient for the current economy; in recent years, the popularization of THC extraction techniques and oil vaporizers has moved marijuana concentrates into the mainstream. And since concentrates can be made out of unsellable plant detritus, processing can turn trash to profit. The market endeavors to provide a nice high on demand with minimal muss and fuss. On the one hand, concentrates appeal to time-pressed teens who are constantly under surveillance and subject to zero-tolerance discipline policies. On the other, these conditions (along with new stoner technology) have turned the communal counterculture ritual of smoking a joint into something closer to medicating with a USB-charging inhaler. It appears that marijuana use—among teens as well as adults—will continue to increase, but as it gets more efficient and scalable, it may not look much like it did in the 1970s. Mainstream magazines have already started running features like "How to Be a Productive Stoner" and "The Productivity Secrets of Wildly Successful Stoners." A few office workers are taking microdoses of LSD on the job for creative enhancement.[45] Does it still count as recreational drug use if you're doing it to work harder?

Aside from marijuana, American teens use controlled substances less than past generations. Among twelfth graders, binge drinking is down by nearly half over the past forty years, as is cigarette smoking. Use of harder illegal drugs like cocaine, meth, LSD, and heroin is down too.[46] No one has a perfect causal analysis, but increased surveillance, heavier penalties, and a lack of public space most likely contribute to the decline, as has the flow of legal (and black-market) pharmaceuticals. (Based on the evidence, however, antidrug propaganda programs like D.A.R.E. don't seem to have been effective.)[47] It might surprise readers to hear that teen heroin use is down, given that we're in the midst of a national opiate crisis, but it's true. Teens were the only age group whose rate of heroin use declined between 2002 and 2013, according to the Centers for Disease Control and Prevention (CDC), while everyone else saw huge increases.[48] Americans are used to thinking about the correlation of recreational drug use and youth (which continues to exist), but we also need to look at the birth cohort effects.

Growing up in expanding postwar America, Baby Boomers (born between 1946 and 1964) crafted the mold for how following generations have imagined "youth," and many of our media stereotypes about teens and young adults flow from the Boomer experience. This is no surprise given the age cohort that owns and manages media companies. But Boomers are their own special group of Americans, with their own predilections. The *Wall Street Journal* broke down the numbers on accidental drug overdoses over time by age and didn't find a consistent pattern: In the early 1970s, fifteen-to-twenty-four-year-olds overdosed most, then it was young and middle-aged adults, and now the forty-five-to-sixty-four-year-olds have taken over.[49] It didn't make much sense, until they looked at how the Boomer cohort traveled through those numbers.

Birth cohort is a better explanatory variable for accidental drug overdoses than age, which is to say that it's not that young people like drugs, it's that Boomers—whether seventeen or seventy—have tended to use drugs more than other cohorts. The overdose rate for the fifty-five-to-seventy-four cohort quintupled between 2001 and 2013 as Boomers aged into that range. Experts concluded that the spike in elderly drug abuse is due to "the confluence of two key factors: a generation with a predilection for mind-altering substances growing older in an era of widespread opioid painkiller abuse."[50] Drug overdoses are no longer a youth phenomenon. Millennials are suffering from the overprescription of drugs (including pain pills), but we aren't the Oxy generation.

Why are Millennials so comparatively sober? Given the historically high stakes for their choices, given how much work they've put into accumulating human capital, perhaps today's young people are more conservative when it comes to taking chances with their brain chemistry. Whatever the reasons, survey data indicates that Millennials were the first wave in a trend of American teens assessing the risks and just saying no at a higher rate than their predecessors.

Drugs aren't the only vice that American teens are declining with increasing frequency. Don't believe what you hear about "hookup culture"; kids are having less sex than they have at any time since the sexual revolution. An article in the journal *Pediatrics* ("Sexual Initiation, Contraceptive Use, and Pregnancy Among Young Adolescents") looked at when young people first have sex based on their birth year. Between 1939 and 1979, an individual was more likely in general to have sex at a younger age than one born the year before.[51] The median age of sexual initiation dropped from nineteen to seventeen during the forty years, while the age at which the youngest 10 percent had sex shrank similarly from just under sixteen to just over fourteen. American teen depravity hit its inflection point in the early 1990s. In just over a decade, the median age of first sexual contact was almost back up to eighteen. According to CDC's Youth Risk Behavior Survey (YRBS) of high schoolers, the average teen now graduates a virgin, a landmark shift that occurred between 1995 and 1997.[52]

As teens are waiting longer to have sex, they're also more responsible once they decide to do it. The Guttmacher Institute—the foremost research think tank when it comes to family planning and reproductive health—found that the number of teens using contraceptives when they first have sex has increased markedly, from under half in 1982 to just under 80 percent by 2011–2013.[53] The teenage birthrate and abortion rate are both down as a result.[54] As with drug use, there's no way to isolate a single cause for elevated rates of teen abstinence. One thing we can rule out is religiosity; Millennials report less faith — both belief and worship — than other American age cohorts.[55] If Millennials are more risk-averse than past generations, then they might be less willing to roll the dice when it comes to an unplanned pregnancy or sexually transmitted infection, but they seem to have found a way to mitigate these risks with contraception. Perhaps increased anxiety and depression means decreased teen libidos, or maybe it's a side effect of the medication. A decline in unsupervised free time probably contributes a lot. At a basic level, sex at its best is unstructured play with friends, a category of experience that the time diaries in Chapter 1 tell us has been decreasing for American adolescents. It takes idle hands to get past first base, and today's kids have a lot to do.

Another contributing cause to the decline of adolescent sexual initiation is a decline in sexual assault and abuse perpetrated against children. A 2006 meta-analysis in the *Journal of Social Issues* mapped out the reduction in maltreatment on a number of different surveys, and though the authors have trouble finding a cause, crimes against children had fallen significantly since the early 1990s.[56] On the National Child Abuse and Neglect Data System measure, the physical and sexual abuse rate had fallen by more than half between 1992 and 2010.[57] Juvenile (ages twelve to seventeen) victimization (on the National Crime Victimization Survey) is down across the board, with the (reported) sexual assault of teens down by over two-thirds during the last twenty years.[58] On the YRBS, the percentage of high schoolers reporting sex before age thirteen (nearly synonymous with abuse) dropped from 10.2 percent in 1991 to 5.6 percent in 2013.[59]

Though there is good reason to believe that these statistics vastly undercount the real rate of sexual assault, these numbers force a reevaluation of the data on teen sexuality, and a confrontation with the hard reality that a significant percentage of early sexual contact is unwanted.[60] The sexual revolution's claim was that with more control over their bodies, young people would be free to explore their sexuality. The stigmas about teen sexuality continue to fall, but more sexual freedom — especially for young women — now correlates with less sex and fewer partners. It's impossible to extricate the trend from confounding variables like declining free time, and with the reporting rates for rape so low, the federal studies are only measuring the tip of an iceberg, but perhaps the longstanding stereotype of teens as sexually obsessed isn't as true as *American Pie* would have us believe. Maybe given the autonomy to choose, more teens are choosing to wait.

That teens are waiting longer to have sex and have fewer partners on average hasn't stopped adults from panicking. The country's nervous parents have focused their anxiety on a relatively new sexual practice: sexting. Armed with camera phones, it's no surprise that teens have started sending each other naked pics, but what to them is a normal sexual practice sounds like self-produced child porn to adults. The best research into actual teen sexting behaviors comes from teams led by Jeff Temple, a professor of obstetrics and gynecology at the University of Texas. In 2012, a team of his interviewed 948 diverse public high school students in southeast Texas about their sexting activity and found a high rate of sexting, with 28 percent reporting having sent a sext and 31 percent reporting having asked for one.[61]

I expect that the rates will increase as camera phones are more universally adopted and app builders like Snap attempt to mitigate the risks of sexting on the technology side, but it's already a mainstream practice. A second study from a Temple-led Texas team looked at the longitudinal association between sexting and sexual behavior and found no connection between sexting and "high-risk" practices (unprotected sex, multiple partners, alcohol and drug use before sex), suggesting that sexting isn't just for "bad" kids.[62] Instead, the study confirmed that some kids were sexting *before* having sex, reversing the older generation's relationship with self-produced nudes. No wonder adults are so confused. Still, the biggest correlate in Temple's studies was between sexting and an ongoing sexual relationship. When Palfrey and Gasser write in *Born Digital* (from a self-described adult perspective) of teen sexting, "Rarely do these stories end well," they are flatly incorrect.[63]

6.5 Porn

Maybe the adults protest too much. Though the stats indicate that fewer children are being sexually abused by adults, that doesn't mean adults have stopped sexualizing young men and especially women. It's mostly adults who are profiting from hypersexualized teen performers. The fashion industry, which is always hustling to stay ahead of the sexy curve, remains fixated on youth and starts the average model working before she turns seventeen.[64] Millions of Internet pornography sites make billions in annual domestic revenue, disproportionately off actors pretending to be kids. As part of a collaboration with *BuzzFeed,* the site Pornhub looked into its metrics and found that "teen" was both the most popular category and search term for male users.[65] "Teen" refers in a strict sense mostly to minors, and the industry term "barely legal" harkens back to Chris Rock's joke about the minimum wage: If they could sell pornographic movies of sixteen-year-olds, they would, but it's illegal. At the intersection of youth, sex, and technology there's a lot of adult anxiety, but there's also a lot of adult profit.

Millennials have grown up in a post–sexual revolution American culture, where *Playboy* yielded to shinier and more mainstream *Maxim,* until both were crushed by Internet porn. For past generations the *Playboy* brand stood in part for the stolen copies hidden under teenage beds; now the magazine can hardly decide whether to even bother with nudity. There is no newsstand operator as easy to sneak by as the online "Don't go to this site if you're not 18" pop-up "barriers." It's hard to get solid data on young people viewing online pornography, in part because it's technically against the law. Porn sites can't exactly tell researchers what percentage of their users they believe to be underage, though as proprietors they have the most reliable ways of tracking their own user demographics. With that caveat, the data we do have suggests that most kids looking at porn on the Internet are over fourteen; the epidemic of sex-crazed ten-year-olds hasn't materialized.[66] Still, most teens have probably looked. Have they suffered from it? The results from a longitudinal study of teens age thirteen to seventeen and online sexual behavior suggest not:

> In general, youth who reported participation in online sexual activities were no better or worse off than those who did not report online sexual activities in terms of sexual health outcomes. Specifically, there were no differences in their rated trust for health care professionals, approach to health care, regular use of health care providers, pregnancy knowledge, STI knowledge, condom and contraception consistency, and fears of STIs. They had comparable levels of communication about sex with their parents and with their sex partners. They also were comparable in terms of levels of self-esteem and self-efficacy, as well as

body image and weight management efforts. There were also no differences between the two groups in their feelings about school, their ability to get along with parents and peers in school, or performance in school. They had similar levels of ratings of the importance of finishing high school, going to college or university, and getting a good job.[67]

Considering the understandable fears about every kid with an Internet connection having easy access to a lot more explicit sexual content than existed in the world a generation ago, that is a whole lot of nothing when it comes to damage. This is only one study, and who knows how virtual reality will change the landscape, but Millennials do not seem to have been irredeemably malformed by the proliferation of online porn, as some commentators have long prophesied. Though it has most likely affected some sexual norms, so did *Playboy*.

On the production end, however, pornography has followed some of the same labor trends we've seen throughout the book. Even in an industry where performers can't legally get started until they hit eighteen, amateurs have supplanted the professionals. The most popular places to see porn are so-called tube sites, as in YouTube. Users upload clips, whether self-produced or pirated. It's like the music industry, but more intense. Professionals have to compete for attention against every exhibitionist with a video camera, and we've seen what kind of effect that dynamic has on wages. In a piece for *The New Yorker*, Katrina Forrester describes how the industry has changed:

> Much online porn is amateur and unregulated. It's hard to tell how much, because there's little data, and even larger studios now ape the amateur aesthetic, but applications for porn-shoot permits in Los Angeles County reportedly fell by ninety-five per

cent between 2012 and 2015. Now most films have low production values, and they are often unscripted. Sometimes you can hear the director's voice; apparently, many viewers can make do without the old fictional tropes of doctors and nurses, schoolgirls, and so on — the porn industry itself having become the locus of fantasy. Where performers like [Jenna] Jameson had multi-film contracts with studios like Wicked or Vivid Entertainment, such deals are now rare, and most performers are independent contractors who get paid per sex act.[68]

Increased competition leads to low-cost, rationalized labor; Millennials know the deal. Increased competition also means profit for someone, and the someone when it comes to porn is a company called MindGeek. "RedTube," "YouPorn," and "Pornhub" sound like competing sites that do the same thing, but that's only half right. All three are owned by MindGeek, which, starting in 2006, began acquiring as many porn networks and production studios as it could get its weird-name-having hands on. MindGeek produces the professional media (that is, the stuff that isn't genuinely user-generated) under one set of labels, and soaks up the ad revenue from pro and amateur content alike by running ads on the tube sites. *Slate*'s David Auerbach described the situation as being as if "Warner Brothers also owned the Pirate Bay."[69] It's a no-lose proposition for management, and a no-win one for labor. Sound familiar?

Conclusion

Cameron: We're screwed.

Michael: No, hey, hey, no, I don't want to hear that defeatist attitude. I want to hear you upbeat!

Cameron: We're screwed!

— 10 Things I Hate About You *(1999)*

In the preceding six chapters, I've tried to give some structural context for the development of the Millennial character. As Jean Twenge writes, *when* we're born into a society has a large impact on our personality. We are products of our environment: country, family, but also era. American Millennials come from somewhere — we didn't emerge fully formed from the crack in an iPhone screen. Tracking the changes in the institutions that have the most influence on children's development gives us more clarity into kids' lives than trying to generalize from cherry-picked behaviors that adults find unnerving. Major national trends like the increase in average worker output, rationalization, downward pressure on the cost of labor, mass incarceration, and elevated competition have shaped a generation of jittery kids teetering on the edge between outstanding achievement and spectacular collapse. What we've seen over the past few decades is not quite a sinister sci-fi plot to shape a cohort of supereffective workers who are too competitive, isolated, and scared to organize for something better, but it has turned out a lot like that.

So far, things are going pretty well for people who own companies or shares of companies. Profits are up, labor costs are down; unions are on their back feet and workers are more productive; there's more inequality, and more jails to house people from the wrong side in case they get any bright ideas. The institutions that sort American children don't necessarily care who wins and who loses—anyone can *technically* climb from the bottom to the top of the national caste system, and it's *possible* to fall from the top to the bottom—but the number of podium spots is determined by larger forces than individual effort or merit. Like Calvinists who thought the heaven-bound were preordained but unknown, everyone has to act as if they are saved, even though most are damned.

Whatever problems they encounter along the way, the public and private institutions we have set up are equipped to function indefinitely into the future. The collapse of the housing market and the 2008 financial crisis smudged the rose-colored glasses, but to the surprise of some commentators, owners were once again able to shift the costs onto the backs of workers. Housing prices are back where they were, and rents are up. We are only in the early days of the Donald Trump administration, but the expected market collapse that was to follow the election of the nation's least-qualified candidate to its highest office hasn't come. That tells me that Trump's promises to shake up the political and economic establishments aren't about to be fulfilled. The social tendencies I've described may be intolerable or unsustainable, but that doesn't necessarily mean they're going to stop happening to us.

Seven Signs of the Bad Future

One of the most difficult things we have to imagine is how the national situation will change if the trends we've examined continue. As in the composition of generations, quantitative change eventually becomes qualitative change. The America that Millennials will eventually lead will be unrecognizable to our grandparents' generation, not simply because of all the technological development or climate change, but also because our basic social relations will be different. Soon "Millennial" won't refer to those rascally kids with their phones, it will be the dominant character of a new America. And it probably won't be pretty.

No single drastic change has to occur; this is the path we've already taken. If we keep going the way we are now, if we extend out the graphs for another few decades, some seriously wild shit will happen. Here are seven slow-motion disasters I fear many of us can look forward to in our lifetimes:

1. Human Capital Contracts

We've seen how central workers' ability to work has become to the economy, and to the lives of young Americans. Human capital is the government's largest financial asset and the population's largest source of debt that isn't backed by land. But right now, with the student lending system nationalized, private capital is more or less locked out of the market. Capitalists could invest in workers as employees, but that's risky, as employees are free to go work elsewhere. What they want is to invest in workers as *capital,* to get a return no matter where the worker works, the way the government gets returns on student loans now. And if they invest in the next Zuckerberg, they want a piece of that multibillion-dollar upside, not just a 4 percent return.

It will begin with a few very-well-qualified students: math prodigies from working-class families or athletes bound for the pros, say. The federal government offers the same loan rates to everyone regardless of their promise, but these top-rated kids are better investments.

Why should they live poor in their twenties if they're going to be rich for the rest of their lives? Algorithms will point lenders to the right kids, and the capitalists will make them better offers than the government can. When lenders start demanding a percentage of future earnings from borrowers in return for money up front it will seem sensible, a private version of Pay As You Earn tailored to individuals.

For the first few cohorts, I imagine these human capital loans will be genuinely win-win: better than student loans for the borrowers, and invigorating for the economy. But as investment sprints into this new space, the standards will decline. The student loan system treats everyone as equal, but that can't possibly hold. First it's Harvard students at 1 percent of your lifetime income, then it's Boston University at 5 percent, University of Maryland at 10. By the time we get to what investors will consider the bottom half of kids, I don't want to think about the percentage of their future income the lenders will require. But those students will still need the start-up money, no matter the future cost. Get used to the idea of "subprime human capital."

2. Professionalization of Childhood

As the entry costs continue increasing and competition keeps intensifying, more American parents will look at the odds, look at their small child, and decide not to enter them in the game. Even middle- and upper-middle-class families will point their kids toward specific careers from a young age, and I don't mean star quarterbacks and violinists. (I can't pretend to know what future livable jobs will look like, but I guess a high proportion of them will involve servicing robots.) The default goal of doing better than the last generation will change; adolescents will hope not to be too much worse off than their parents.

The calculations and projections about student debt and future income we require teenagers and their families to make now will become more complicated, but their conclusions will be, perhaps, more direct. Instead of encouraging every child to be all they can be and imagine themselves rich and famous, the authorities will start to talk about everyone "finding a place" in society.

Once again, for some kids, this will be an improvement. Making school blatantly preprofessional dispenses with nice fuzzy liberal notions of what education is for, but it's easy to see how a childhood spent preparing for a secure career in, say, home electronics repair might be more enjoyable than being set up to fail in a giant contest for a tiny number of really good lives. Compared to the levels of anxiety and work it will take to compete at the highest levels, having a path chosen for them may come as a relief.

At that point, however, America is basically an explicit hereditary caste system, the one thing we've always claimed we're not. We won't tell every child they can be anything they set their mind to, because that will sound ridiculous. Not even a kid will be able to believe it.

3. Climate Privilege

Here are two things we know for sure about global warming: It's real and we're not stopping it. We humans—and Americans in particular—have made irrevocable changes to the ecosystem that have destabilized the climate. Arguing about those facts while sea ice melts is ridiculous. The Environmental Protection Agency predicts the following between now and 2100, basically regardless of what we do from this point on: a national 3°F to 12°F increase in temperature, with extremely hot summers; an increased prevalence of exceptionally heavy rainstorms and hurricanes; a 15 percent decrease in American snow cover and a foot increase in sea level; and a decrease in coral production over 50 percent.[1] *Fuck,* right?

But nothing is experienced by everyone the same way, not even the weather. The market will price insulation from the climate crisis just like it prices everything else. The rich—and the people they need around—will live in relatively hospitable areas, while the poor will live on the edges of habitability. As automation progresses, the rich won't need the poor so physically close. They could live in whole separate climates.

More than the rural-suburban-urban divide, zones of climate intensity will structure the domestic movement of populations. This will include increased regulation of homelessness and vagrancy, so as to prevent freeloaders from enjoying the temperate zones. I'm not sure if the guards will be robots or humans (or, more likely, what combination of the two), but there will be a lot of gates. For a while we'll comment on how weird it is that our behavior is so strongly determined by the weather, and then we won't anymore.

4. Discrimination by Algorithm

One of twentieth-century America's greatest self-proclaimed feats was the elimination of officially sanctioned discrimination. Man, woman, black, white: No matter who you are, you are now supposedly equally entitled to public services and accommodations, as well as whatever private ones you can afford. Women can get credit cards and mortgages—if they're eligible. And it's illegal to put in a covenant when you sell your house saying the buyers can't sell it to nonwhites. We are, as a nation, very proud of this accomplishment, even if it's uneven and unfinished.

But as with the reduction of elder poverty, we may have mistaken a cyclical dip for a permanent accomplishment.

As so much of American social and economic life has migrated online, we don't really know how well any of our antidiscrimination codes are holding. The more advanced an enterprise, the more it can tailor the individual customer experience. When I look at Amazon.com while I'm logged in to my account, I don't necessarily see the same prices you do. How exactly Amazon determines who sees what is not only incomprehensibly complicated to nonexperts, it's a constantly evolving corporate secret. Innovation has triumphed over regulation, and people are voting for Amazon with their dollars. We don't honestly know if they or any other online vendors are offering better prices to, say, white customers. But it's a fact that discrimination that was explicitly disallowed has wandered through the tech back door — it was recently discovered that Facebook was letting users target ads for housing by race.[2]

I don't think regulators will be able to catch up, and in a world based on individual customer profiles, the idea of ending discrimination will seem quaint. The algorithms see us less as individuals than as confluences of probabilities. We don't have races per se, we have "ethnic affiliations" based on how our observed behavior compares to large data sets of other people's observed behavior. Americans will understand less and less the exact ways in which we're being profiled and discriminated against (or in favor of), and even when we do know, we'll have a hard time proving it. Human capital lenders won't have to add race — give them enough proxy metrics (think of how racially coded arrest records are based on the data in Chapter 4, for example) and they'll be able to figure it out most of the time. To every accusation of discrimination, they'll be able to respond, "No, that's just you."

We will come to understand that every interaction each of us has with a computer system is also a statement about our value as individuals, as measured by stereotyping. This will (understandably) drive us mad.

5. The Malfunctioning

More people will be unable to keep up with the baseline demands of American society. Some will experience mental breaks as they're pushed past prime productivity levels; others won't be able to find a place in the labor pool and will become estranged from mainstream society. Another group will be labeled crazy because they'll be unwilling to tolerate the various trends we've already discussed and will strike out violently or unpredictably. Of course, all of these types of people exist now, but we don't deal with them in a unified way, except through the criminal justice system. And I don't think that imprisonment (as we think about it now) will be able to scale to the necessary level.

America will need institutions for people who just can't make it. Based on the trends as I read them, I don't think this will be "funemployment" on a guaranteed minimum income. It's more likely to be an unholy combination of mental asylum and work camp. These places will seem humane compared to prison or living untreated on the streets, and the move into them will probably be sold to the public (and the families of captives) as caring reform. They'll be breeding grounds for private-public partnerships, with their captive, choiceless consumers and pools of potential labor.

My real fear is that authorities will find a way to break down the perceptual distinction between being alive and doing work. Maybe it will be *Black Mirror*'s rows of treadmills, but I'm thinking more like very advanced video game design. Tech enthusiast Shane Snow controversially suggested that we'd be better off if prison inmates were just sucking on Soylent dispensers and living through Oculus headsets.[3] Giving asylum inmates games to play all day will seem generous, and if we can somehow extract value from their playing (the way Google uses CAPTCHA verification to gather street addresses for their Maps program), then it's a win-win, at least compared to incarceration as it exists. This puts us on the *Matrix* path, where living in reality is itself a privilege.

6. Misogynist Backlash

Starting in 1977 and continuing yearly after 1985, the NORC research corporation has conducted the General Social Survey, as a part of which they have asked Americans four questions in particular about gender relations. Three are about women working outside the home, one is about whether men are more emotionally suited for politics. In 1977, fewer than 50 percent surveyed took the progressive position on any of the questions, but by 2012, every question scored at 65 percent or above.[4] Millennial attitudes reflect this social turning point; most of us have always believed that women could perform wage labor without destroying families.

However, 35 percent is still a lot, and it's not evenly distributed. All things being equal, the less education an American has, the lower they score on these gender equality questions. That makes sense, and not because we learn gender equality in college. More than an index of knowledge, education is a proxy for success in the contemporary labor market. (Not that all college graduates do great, but they're generally doing better than those who don't graduate from high school.) I think the past correlation between a larger share of GDP going to labor and women's low participation has turned and will turn to causation in some minds. As job polarization intensifies, I fear an increasing number of Americans will blame feminists, working women, and just women in general.

Among currently surveyed age cohorts, Millennials hold the most progressive attitudes with regard to gender equality, and we're the first generation to grow up holding these as majority views. Which is good. But I worry that misogyny will acquire a countercultural sheen. Hatred for women could replace hatred for Jews as what Ferdinand Kronawetter called the "socialism of fools" and confound efforts to clarify what is really happening to American working people. If that happens, the Millennial legacy will be very different from the progressive vision with which we began.

7. Fully Tracked

With the right authorizations, an interested party could find out anything they want to know about me. Whom I've talked to, when, about what. Every single place I've been for years. Whatever I've bought or thought about buying. All of my work, ever. What the theorist Rob Horning calls the "data self" is continually approaching the real self, especially when it comes to Millennials like me who don't leave the house without our phones. I don't have a fitness tracker that keeps constant tabs on my body, but lots of people do, and more will.

This vast tracking apparatus is already being used to guide our behavior in innumerable ways, but I believe both sides will become increasingly open about the arrangement. The data self is an amazing accountability tool, and as tech developers race beyond the regulators' imaginations, I think government will take the "if you can't beat them…" tack. Public-private tech partnerships will become the norm, with corporations willing to trade safety from the law and big contracts for some good branding and policy collaboration. And it will be presented to the people as a bargain.

Here's how: Right now, my health insurance (bought on the Pennsylvania Obamacare exchange) gives me $150 toward a gym membership. Healthy insurees make for low costs; it's a win-win. But to get that subsidy, I have to comply with onerous reporting requirements to confirm that I actually go to the gym. I don't bother, and I don't imagine a ton of other people do either. But if we were offered free Fitbits to wear to the gym, the barriers would fall. Nothing about that sounds bad necessarily, but all of a sudden we're in a world where people are hurrying to the gym so they can run long and hard enough to afford their health insurance.

These are some of the major changes that will happen if nothing changes. None of them is a huge leap from what's already come to pass; some would say everything on this list has already happened, which is true to a certain extent. But over the next couple of decades, I believe we'll see some quantitative-to-qualitative jumps, in which today's normal is superseded by a new way of life. I predict the transitions will be more or less smooth, not in terms of human suffering, but in terms of social and political stability. And barring a revolution, these may be the kinds of major changes that define our generation.

There is a seam between here and there—lines we will cross—but we probably won't recognize them until we're on the other side. We don't know how the Millennial generation will be remembered, but when I think about this list, I'm not confident we'll like it. Think about the Baby Boomers: They were proud of their (comparatively) broad experimentations with drugs as part of their resistance to stolid midcentury American culture, and though I've never seen the appeal of *Easy Rider,* some of their pride seems justified. However, in the long run, their age cohort's relationship to drugs will probably be defined by some members' willingness to poison the others to death with pills for money. I don't think that's what Boomers were shooting for (so to speak), but it was a somewhat predictable outcome in retrospect. I'm not warning that everyone "sells out" when they get older; my point is that every birth cohort confronts real and specific historical challenges, and our better angels sometimes lose.

So what can Millennials do to avoid becoming the nightmare version of ourselves? If we don't want to live in a dystopia, how can we step off this path and go somewhere else? After all, books like this are supposed to end with a solution, right?

Bop It Solutions

Is it even possible to change the path we're on? Based on the evidence so far, it sounds difficult. According to conventional wisdom, our society has a number of mechanisms and apparatuses through which we can bend its operation to our popular will. If we are unhappy with the way this country is managed, with its priorities, with its distribution of resources and feelings—as so many of us seem to be—we should be able to change them. Isn't America a democracy? At the very least, we have consumer choices. I believe it is worth the time to think through some of the blueprints for change we have at hand.

In 1996, when I was seven years old, Hasbro released a toy called Bop It. A plastic stick featuring a button in the middle and knobs on the ends, Bop It directed players, through a speaker, to fiddle with one of three parts depending on the command: Twist one knob ("Twist it!"), pull the other ("Pull it!"), or bop the center button ("Bop it!"). It sounds easy, but like a tongue twister, it gets harder the longer and faster you go. (A couple of years later Hasbro introduced the Bop It Extreme with additional "Flick it!" and "Spin it!" commands; the 2010 Bop It XT added "Shake it!"). I mention the game not just as another example of our tendency toward accelerating difficulty and complexity in childhood tasks, but because Bop It is a good metaphor for how social change is supposed to work under the present system. If we want to make a change, we select a move from the menu: Buy It!, Vote It!, Give It!, Protest It! Just as soon as you do one, another cycles around. The series doesn't have an end.

In the conclusions of books like this one, authors tend to land on some sequence of those moves: Buy It! Vote It! Or Give It! Protest It! No matter how deep and intractable the problems laid out by the writer, some combination of these tactics *sounds* like it should be able to address them. At the very least, calling out some progressive Bop It moves gives a bummed-out text an end that's distinct from the preceding pile of despair. "The people united can never be defeated," and it might be true, but a reminder that a change or solution is always still possible usually functions as a cop-out. Following hundreds of pages of focused analysis with Bop It—no matter how soaring the rhetoric—feels almost dishonest. Instead, I'm going to look at these concluding strategies (consumer politics, electoral engagement, charitable giving, and expressive protest) one by one and see where they actually go, rather than suggesting where it's possible they might lead under a set of imaginary circumstances.

For Millennials, wide-ranging social change is a material question. Every generation has a historical window when its members are tasked with directing the country, and we are just beginning ours. If Millennials are going to alter the path we're on, it's realistically going to happen in the next ten to twenty years. That's a limited time frame in which to get from here (which is to say, everything I've described up until now—a path to dystopia) to anywhere else. The series of historical disasters that I've outlined, the one that characterizes my generation, is a big knot. There's not a single thread we can pull to undo it, no one problem we can fix to make sure the next generation grows up happier and more secure. The Bop It moves are holistic, their ranges are wide, and their potential impacts are profound. But if they're going to work beyond an academic or a theoretical conversation, they also have to be *plausible* for *us*.

1. Buy It!

Say there are some of us who want to change the world in a positive way. We want poor people near or far to have more than they have now. We want women's equality and respect for trans people and an end to white-supremacist aggression. We want environmental sustainability and/or good jobs. In American society, there is one principal mechanism for the fulfillment of desires: the market. If you want a hamburger, you can buy a hamburger. If you want a $1 hamburger, you can buy it. If you want a $30 hamburger (and have $30 to spend on a hamburger), you can buy one of those too. Theoretically, companies can bake social values into products that consumers can buy. If you want a Christian hamburger, you can get that (if you're in California it's particularly easy), and you can grab some self-identified gay ice cream for dessert in New York.

The market's ostensible purpose is to provide an efficient match between people who want stuff and people who produce stuff to meet those wants. If Americans really want to stop carbon emissions, they will always buy products that are carbon-neutral when available, which will cue producers to change their practices, and then we've done it. We can apply this same consumer logic to any social problem. If movies with women protagonists are objectionably scarce, we can generate a virtuous cycle by backing up our values with our dollars. In this vision, our society is incredibly democratic: Each of us trades our time and effort for votes on how everything works, which we cast by spending. Sometimes when I see certain advertisements I think people really believe this is how the world works. But it's not.

It is true that there exists an interplay between consumers and producers; some of the owners even let us help decide which potato chip flavors we get to buy. But our choices are very limited, and not just by the selection on the shelves. With few exceptions, Americans either own companies or have to work for those who do. The main use of money isn't expressing our values, it's buying the things we need—like food and shelter—in order to stay alive and participate in society. You don't *need* to pay for a cell phone plan; there's no law. It sure helps if you want a job or friends, however. There is, of course, an ethical-branded cell phone provider, but I'm not a customer. Aside from the general corniness with which these companies pursue their idea of politics, they suffer from some obvious disadvantages. Because it tends to cost money to have values—the cheapest way to make something is probably not the kindest or most sustainable—ethical products tend to cost more. (For example, when I was a politically engaged teenager I wanted the *Adbusters* ethical Converse sneaker replacement, but they were three times more expensive.) That turns political engagement into a luxury people will pay for, and that encourages companies to fake it.

I don't mean that company founders pretend to hold certain beliefs in order to make their products more appealing, though I'm sure that happens on occasion. I mean that companies will use public relations tools (some no more expensive than a social media intern) and branding to wrap themselves in the aura of values. After all, if people are willing to pay more to feel like they're enacting their politics, then it's worth selling it to them, just as long as it costs less than the premium they're willing to pay. From there it's a race to the bottom. Buying a product branded as ethical actually *encourages* this cycle, heightening the incentives for companies to look (rather than be) good. A label race prods marketers to invent and exhaust evocative standards like "organic" or "carbon-neutral" or "GMO-free." This whole mess makes it hard to distinguish between a product that promotes a set of values and a product that uses a set of values to promote itself. The commercialization of politics becomes its own problem, and it's hard to buy your way out of that. Millennials know how to play this game — who, after all, is writing the promotional tweets? — and it's embittering.

Millennials have been raised on consumer politics. In her 1995 study *Doing Their Share to Save the Planet,* sociologist Donna Lee King examined early-1990s environmentalist rhetoric directed at children and how the kids themselves interpreted it. At the time, environmentalism was just beginning to come into vogue, and companies saw a branding opportunity. Since then, depoliticized save-the-earth rhetoric has been used to sell everything from hamburgers to sport utility vehicles. Pollution became a villain, the kind that superheroes could punch in the face, but when kids tried to join in the fight, they were redirected to bottles of ranch dressing branded with Captain Planet. This is about as mixed a message as you can give kids; as King describes it: "Children are encouraged to be aware of global environmental problems, are provided with simple lifestyle solutions, and then are roundly criticized for demanding the most minor changes in patterns of family consumption."[5]

It's on a more fundamental level that the whole enterprise of ethics through consumerism is a waste of time. The market is not a magic desire-fulfilling machine we can reprogram to green the earth and level inequality. It is, rather, a vast system of exploitation in which workers are compelled to labor for their subsistence, and owners reap the profits. The market offers a variety of goods and experiences that seems infinite, but it's actually very limited. There are many different flavors of Pop-Tarts, but none of them opens a portal to a world where you don't have to trade half your waking life to get enough to eat.

At the end of the day, trying to improve society with consumerism is like stepping up to the plate and trying to throw a touchdown. You're playing the wrong game. The market is built to generate profit, and though there might be room for the occasional high-minded hippie co-op, they are the exception. Businesses that plan to make big profits the old-fashioned way—exploitation—can attract capital investment, giving them an insurmountable leg up on the little guys. As Joe Strummer put it, "Selling is what selling sells," and selling isn't going to sell itself out.

It is theoretically conceivable that everyone will get together and decide only to buy products from companies that pay high wages, halting or reversing many of the trends I've described so far. It's also theoretically conceivable that, as you read this, a large meteor is headed our way and will strike the earth and obliterate all life before you get the chance to finish this conclusion. A reasonable observer should conclude that the latter is much more likely.

2. Vote It!

The free market isn't the only mechanism we have that's supposed to respond to our collective desires. This is a democracy (at least at the time of this writing), and if we don't like our national policies or priorities, if they aren't in our collective interest (and they don't seem to be), then we can vote the bums out. No matter how entrenched the powers that be, the American people are ultimately sovereign, and we always hold a big enough crowbar to pry them out of place. And if we don't like any of the politicians on offer, any of us can put ourselves up for office, either through a party primary or through an independent bid. The system is infinitely adaptable according to the will of the people, and it has survived the Civil War, the expansion of the franchise to women, segregation, Vietnam and the antiwar movement. American society has undergone major upheavals, but our political system works like a set of shock absorbers, flexing and contracting to fit people's needs. And when things get *really* bad or complicated, there's even an emergency switch: The Constitution itself can be amended.

And yet, despite such an ostensibly flexible system, most people aren't very happy with their government. According to the Pew Research Center, the portion of Americans who trust the government to do the right thing most of the time is below 20 percent, a nearly unique low in the organization's then fifty-seven-year history of asking the question.[6] It's an enduring and bipartisan trend, one that fluctuates based on the party in power less than you might imagine. Despite some big talk about government transparency in the age of the Internet, the American state seems less accountable to its people than ever before—insofar as people are unhappy with their representation and aren't able to rectify that. Either our democratic institutions aren't functioning the way we're told they're supposed to, or Americans aren't using them. Or it's some combination of the two.

The best answer here is probably the simplest, and it's one most Americans already know and probably even believe: The government is rigged, man. Pew's report about public mistrust had 74 percent saying politicians put themselves first and 55 percent saying ordinary

Americans would do a better job. We are unhappy with our rulers and think we could do better. In a democracy, this is supposed to be great news! Now we get to send Mr. Smith to Washington to clean house and expose the system's evil machinations.

While I wrote this book, Donald Trump pulled off an improbable ascent to the White House based on a funhouse performance of the reform narrative. He was a man of the people, he was headed to Washington to "drain the swamp." Against any candidate other than Hillary Clinton, Trump's antiauthoritarian pose probably would have faltered, but the Democratic primary is structured to the advantage of establishment candidates, and no third-party figure stood a chance in the general. Now we get a con man's reforms: All of the rhetoric, none of the substance.

For a long time some progressives have argued that campaign finance reform is the silver bullet for all that ails the American political system. If we locked big money out, the people would be free to pick representatives to represent our interests (including the nationalization of the health care system, say, and protections for labor unions). The people's government would drive the cost of living down and the price of labor up. Society would share collectively in the benefits of technological development. Capitalism and exploitation would melt away over time like disappearing legs on an evolving whale.

It sounds like a good plan, but when you think about it, it's a little bit like trying to jump by pulling on your shoelaces. If the people had the kind of control of the state apparatus necessary to pass a constitutional amendment (or a policy of its power and significance) to disconnect economic and political power, then we wouldn't need the reform in the first place! Call it the Bernie Sanders paradox: If he could be elected president, then we wouldn't need to elect him president. And yet the Senate's sole socialist, Sanders, spent over $200 million in his quixotic 2016 primary campaign, more than enough to compete. It wasn't lack of money that cost the left-wing populist the election; he also had the powerful elements of the Party arrayed against him. Money is power, but cash on hand is not the *only* kind of power. A lasting solution to the problem of big money in politics, then, seems both implausible in the near term and not necessarily effective even if we achieved it. It's no silver bullet. After all, Donald Trump was outspent by Hillary Clinton two to one.[7]

Like consumer politics, the electoral system isn't actually built to enact the will of the people. That's why people don't feel like the government acts in their interests: It doesn't. American politics is a professional realm, and most people aren't invited to do much more than raise their hands every couple of years. Many don't even bother with the hand-raising part. Given what we know about the work lives of nonrich Americans, with what time and resources are they (on a massive scale) supposed to get involved in politics? A certain percentage of folks at all income levels will take to activism, but electoral politics has high barriers to entry. Without a genuine labor party, working-class Americans don't have a reliable path that leads inside, and the professional incumbents have huge advantages when it comes to maintaining their positions. For most people, disengagement with electoral politics is only logical.

It is possible that as the entire Millennial cohort reaches voting age, we will run candidates of our own whose ideas about how the country should be run are drastically different from the incumbents'. Millennials will be the largest generational voting demographic in the coming years; maybe a youth-heavy bloc will vote in a wave of politicians who will take global warming and workers' share of production seriously as existential issues to be addressed immediately.[8] But I don't think that's going to happen. Future Millennial politicians—even if most of us haven't met most of them yet—are already well trained in the current ways of doing business, because they're the ones who competed their way to the top. Based on what we've seen about the kind of preparation Millennial professionals receive, our politicians will be *extra* craven, and responsive to an even smaller class of superrich influencers.

The young people who could provide the type of leadership we need—kind, principled, thoughtful, generous, radical, visionary, inspiring—won't touch electoral politics with a ten-foot pole. At least not the ones I've met. To unravel our corrupt political system all the way to the local level and build it back up again with a new vision would take more time—and probably a different country—than we have.

3. Give It!

Just because our major institutions are almost certainly irredeemable in what I see as the crucial near future doesn't mean we can't do *anything*. People don't need institutions to change their society, because people and their interactions *are* society. If we decided to treat each other better, we could have a whole new world without having to infiltrate and reform the market or electoral politics. We can voluntarily improve our collective situation. Be the change you wish to see in the world; the personal is political: Millennials have seen the bumper stickers and the Apple advertisements. What's more, they seem to be working. While our generational confidence in our state institutions has declined, our sense of personal responsibility has increased.

Comparative survey data from 1984 and 2013 shows a significant increase in the proportion of Americans under thirty who think it's important to volunteer (up from 19 to 29 percent), as well as those who actually do (up from 14 to 20 percent).[9] The phenomenon of secular volunteerism has grown along with Millennials, and now it's not uncommon for public high schools and universities to require a certain number of volunteer hours for students to graduate. Volunteerism as an ideology and Millennials are a good match. There are opportunities for young people to be of some service in any field they desire, and many of these opportunities can also fit on a résumé. Volunteering (as distinct from simply doing good things) is credentialed and official. It's an activity that slides into one of the nonlabor slots that ostensibly well-rounded twenty-first-century individuals have to fill with passions, hobbies, and extracurriculars.

It is possible to be a professional volunteer—more possible than ever, in fact. According to the Philanthropy Roundtable, the nonprofit sector has been growing as a percentage of American gross domestic product, from under 2 percent in 1950 to 5.6 percent in 2014.[10] That makes sense, since rich people fund nonprofits and rich Americans have done quite well for themselves over that period. It also means that there is a whole other professional field outside government and "ethical" business where people can channel their collectivist spirit within an individualist system without rocking the boat too hard.

I can understand why some people—especially Millennials— really take the volunteerist idea to heart. There's a lot of need for good to be done out there, and all the "business with a mission" rhetoric from the Buy It! section gets into your brain eventually. But the increase in nonprofit activity and volunteering hasn't led to improved life outcomes for the least of us. If anything, the correlation looks like it goes the other way: The more official do-gooders we have, the worse off more people seem to be. As a holistic strategy for social improvement, volunteerism seems to lack a solid empirical foundation. That is to say: It doesn't really work.

That doesn't mean there are no volunteers or nonprofits that do good, important work. I like to think I've worked for a couple of them. Based on my experience, most of the people who work in the nonprofit world aren't dupes. They're doing the best they can to make a positive difference in the world while getting from one month to the next just like everyone else. They're not generally under the impression that their work is going to solve structural problems, and the idea that volunteerism and nonprofit advocacy are our main road forward generally comes from the funders rather than the laborers. At its best, volunteerism is amelioration, and there's only so far that can go.

We have, once again, the wrong tool. "Volunteering" in general doesn't require a commitment to any particular cause or world view. It's easy to imagine a scenario where one student's volunteering with a prolife group cancels out another volunteer's time with a prochoice organization, for example. "Nonprofit" is a tax-code designation, and it includes good and bad. As in ethical product labeling, corporations have caught up with the do-gooders, and it's hard to find a malevolent multinational without a charitable foundation or two of its own. The same business leaders who push down wages, push up competition, and even push dangerous pharmaceuticals would much rather be seen as givers. So when they're done pushing for a minute, they give a bit, and then they talk about it a lot.

Nonprofits rely on the government, corporations, and the class of people that manages all three of them. At the highest levels, the same individuals move effortlessly through all three spheres. (Just ask Hillary Clinton, whose orbit has included the Senate, the board of Walmart, and of course the Clinton Foundation.) Together they operate as a single apparatus, but of the three it's definitely the volunteers (amateur and professional) who are subordinate. A lot of nonprofit work (to the chagrin of most of the people doing it) involves sucking up to rich people—whereas sucking up to the government is called lobbying. And it's the nonprofits that have to scrap everything they're doing and start over when a new political party comes into power.

For the nonprofit sector and its volunteers to force a fundamental change in direction for corporate America and the state itself would be something like a magician's bunny devouring him alive: It would be a stunning reversal in character, for one thing, but more important, a rabbit's mouth is *way* too small. Implausible doesn't begin to describe it. The volunteerism trick is well tailored to Millennials, but anyone who answers your desire for systematic change with a link to a nonprofit jobs board is pulling your leg or the wool over your eyes. Or maybe a fast one. Regardless, they're pulling something.

4. Protest It!

None of our institutions look as if they will transform American society in the ways we'd need them to in order to reverse the trends described in this book. The Founders foresaw the possibility of such a situation, and they built an emergency button into our system. If the American people find our collective situation intolerable—and I believe many of us should and do—and we can't find any recourse in our democratic structures—as I don't believe we can—then we are legally entitled to go outside and yell.

The First Amendment gives us the right to get together and complain until things change or we get too tired to keep going. It's a time-honored American tradition, and though most people don't approve of protesters at the time, the ones who end up being influential get the rose-colored-glasses treatment. The protesters of the civil rights movement are official heroes, as are the suffragists. The twentieth-century women's rights movement is getting there too; antiwar protesters usually start getting credit a few wars later. Protesters for gay marriage helped change the national conversation so fast that we got credit more or less immediately. If things are fucked up and bullshit (as the Occupy Wall Street slogan goes), then the least we can do is say so, and sometimes that's enough.

Protesting is implied by the Constitution, but it isn't within the system, at least not conventionally. The right-wing "Tea Party" protests were funded in part by rich Republican donors, and on the left George Soros has long been accused of fomenting dissent for his own unspecified ends. But most protesters are out on the street because they believe in something and they want the world to change. Like volunteering, protest isn't necessarily linked to any particular ideological agenda—"gay marriage protesters" could mean two different things, for example. The classic examples of successful American protest generally come from the progressive side, however, especially when it comes to large public marches. A classic Bop It–style instruction for Millennials from Baby Boomers is "We stopped the Vietnam War! You just need to get out there [insert a crack about social media here] and make yourselves heard."

Millennials don't have one thing to protest; we have a whole way of life. Occupy Wall Street (and the nationwide protests and occupations that followed) was an attempt to protest the whole knot, and Millennials camped out in major cities around the country. Instead of a demand, we had a complaint: Shit is fucked up and bullshit. Instead of one policy, we had an enemy: the 1 percent, the people who are profiting from popular immiseration. Based on the data, it's a good set of enemies for Millennials to pick, and it was mostly Millennials participating.[11]

Most of us out there protesting didn't think of it like this, but the way we were carefully following the rules was characteristic of our generation. We've been trained to read the instructions to the end and think creatively. We tried to hit the Constitution's emergency button, and we did it by taking advantage of social media and poorly structured rules about the control of public-private spaces. For a while, it worked. People around the world took notice, and the message (mostly) got across. The reverberations are still being felt. But the protests ended, and not because the government wrote off student debt and seized ill-gotten gains from a host of bankers. Some people went home because they got tired, but more joined. What stopped us was the police, whose orders changed. If they decide we can't protest anymore, they can round up many hundreds of us at a time and put us all in cages. Which is pretty much what happened.

Protests aren't always legal. In fact, the police on-scene can basically declare any protest illegal whenever they want. At that point, protesters can try to leave and/or get beaten and/or gassed and/or arrested. American police departments of any significant size at all (and plenty of insignificant size) have the equipment (read: weapons) necessary to disperse and subdue virtually whatever angry and determined crowd they encounter. As long as the police and politicians are willing to brutalize their fellow Americans, that is. (And they are.)

Police departments across the country used the same aggressive strategies and tactics against Black Lives Matter protesters who took to the streets following the unceasing murder of black Americans by the state in 2013. I remain convinced that, had the National Guard not occupied Ferguson, Missouri, the protesters would have overthrown their city government. But the troops rolled in and the demonstrations were put down. We may have an emergency alarm built into the Constitution, but no amendment will wash the pepper spray out of your eyes if you protest longer than the police want you to. That's often the price protesters pay, but they can't do it forever, and there's nothing in our recent history that suggests to me that a move-ment of expressive street demonstrations could outlast the cops and remain effective. Hell, the Iraq War still isn't over, and I started pro-testing that in ninth grade.

If protest is only protest until the authorities decide they don't want to tolerate it anymore, then that's a significant limit on its effective-ness. As distinct from, say, the blockade of the Dakota Access Pipe-line, which was a struggle over the control of territory, protest is about expressing discontent. Even if it's not going to transform American society directly, protest seems important, if only to keep the idea of discontent and dissent alive. But if the people in power are willing to use guns before they will capitulate, then protest is not a plausible road to wide-ranging social change.

5. Put It Down!

Whenever activists do organize well enough to start playing progres-sive Bop It, we find that the instructions keep changing. (That is the game, after all.) FDR once told civil rights activists that they needed to "make me do it" by protesting, a story that former president Obama repeated on the campaign trail (even though it's actually apocryphal). We can't just vote for politicians to do the things we want; we then have to protest to the people we elected to make sure they do the things they said they were going to do. But how can we have any cred-ibility if we're posting about the protest with corporate iPhones or walking in it with Nikes? First we have to put our money where our mouth is and stop supporting the 1 percent's exploitation. But how can we justify spending $135 on ethical, organic hemp sneakers when there are kids with no good shoes at all, and in our own neighbor-hoods? First we should organize a community shoe drive. But how can we think charity can solve structural problems in a society full of them? What we really need to do is elect better representatives. And so on, and so on, and so on.

There's always another move we could be making—that is the entire game. It reminds me of a circular verse from elementary school meant to irritate anyone within listening range: "Crazy? / I was crazy once. / They locked me in a room full of bunnies. / Bunnies? / I hate bunnies. / They drive me crazy. / Crazy?..." Having experienced both, I think progressive Bop It is the less tolerable loop of the two. It's a string of all-purpose objections that leads *nowhere*. Anyone who invites you to start playing is clueless, disingenuous, or both. The only way to win is not to start.

Final Word

Another illusion is that there is not time enough for our work....
A poor Indian chief of the Six Nations of New York made a
wiser reply than any philosopher, to some one complaining that
he had not enough time. "Well," said Red Jacket, "I suppose you
have all there is."

　　　　　　　　　—*Ralph Waldo Emerson, "Works and Days"*

I don't remember a lot of specific lessons from my decade-plus of
math classes (at least not at a conscious level), but I do remember
the intermediate value theorem. The IVT says—simplified—that
any kind of line connecting two points passes through every point
between them. Maybe I remember the lesson because the word
problem we used in class was so poetic. It featured two monks: one
ascending a mountain, the other walking down from the peak.
We had to prove that (as long as they took spiral paths) the two would
collide somewhere, no matter what. The story stuck in my mind,
and sometimes I think of historical events in the same way: As the
Millennial cohort ages and climbs, the descending monk is coming around the bend, sooner or later. We don't know for sure when
or where our crucial moments are coming, but we do know that
they are.

If we're lucky and brave, the generation of American Millennials will be characterized by a choice. Either we continue the trends
we've been given and enact the bad future, or we refuse it and cut the
knot of trend lines that defines our collectivity. We become fascists or

revolutionaries, one or the other. If we find ourselves without luck or bravery, I fear it will seem in retrospect like we never had a choice at all. But, to paraphrase Red Jacket, we'll have all there is. And it is up to the Millennial cohort to make something else of what's been made of us.

Acknowledgments

Special thanks to Adrian, Angus, Anne, Atossa, Bob, Bobbie, Brandon, Cecilia, Chris, Daniel, David, Donna, Ellen, Erin, Evan, Grace, Hannah, JB, JC, Jean, Jo, Jon, Josh, Julia, Juliana, Katelyn, Katie, Laurie, Legba, Lily, Mary, Mary Grace, Max, Mike, Miranda, Monalisa, Morgan, Nick, Rachel, Rob, Rich, Sam, Sarah, Will, Woj, and Zach.

Notes

Chapter 1: Danny Dunn and the Homework Machine

1. Valerie Strauss, "Kindergarten show canceled so kids can keep studying to become 'college and career ready.' Really," *Washington Post,* April 26, 2014.

2. Matthew M. Chingos, "Ending Summer Vacation Is Long Overdue—Here's How to Pay for It," Brookings Institution, August 7, 2013.

3. David Von Drehle, "The Case Against Summer Vacation," *Time,* July 22, 2010.

4. Matthew Yglesias, "Summer Vacation Is Evil," *Slate,* July 24, 2013.

5. Jürgen Zinnecker, "Children in Young and Aging Societies: The Order of Generations and Models of Childhood in Comparative Perspective," in *Children at the Millennium: Where Have We Come From, Where Are We Going?* ed. Sandra L. Hofferth and Timothy J. Owens, Oxford: Elsevier Science Ltd., 2001, p. 45.

6. Jay Williams and Raymond Abrashkin, *Danny Dunn and the Homework Machine,* New York: Scholastic Book Services, 1958, p. 3.

7. Ibid., p. 59.

8. Sandra L. Hofferth and John F. Sandberg, "Changes in American Children's Time, 1981–1997," in *Children at the Millennium: Where Have We Come From, Where Are We Going?* ed. Sandra L. Hofferth and Timothy J. Owens, Oxford: Elsevier Science Ltd., 2001, pp. 203–224.

9. Sandra L. Hofferth, "Changes in American Children's Time—1997 to 2003," *Electronic International Journal of Time Use Research,* Vol. 6, No. 1, 2009, pp. 26–47.

10. Jürgen Zinnecker, "Children in Young and Aging Societies: The Order of Generations and Models of Childhood in Comparative Perspective," in *Children at the Millennium: Where Have We Come From, Where Are We Going?* ed. Sandra L. Hofferth and Timothy J. Owens, Oxford: Elsevier Science Ltd., 2001, p. 45.

11. The College Board, "Annual AP Program Participation 1956–2012," 2012.

12. The College Board, "AP Score Distributions—All Subjects 1992–2012," 2012.

13. Karl Taro Greenfield, "My Daughter's Homework Is Killing Me," *Atlantic,* September 18, 2013.

14. Jay Williams and Raymond Abrashkin, *Danny Dunn and the Homework Machine,* New York: Scholastic Book Services, 1958, p. 42.

15. Executive Office of the President, "Increasing College Opportunity for Low-Income Students," January 2014, p. 3.

16. Gary Becker, "Human Capital: A Theoretical and Empirical Analysis, with Special Reference to Education, 2nd ed," National Bureau of Economic Research, 1975, p. 25.

17. Tamara R. Mose, *The Playdate: Parents, Children, and the New Expectations of Play,* NYU Press, 2016, p. 144.

18. Singh, G. K., *Child Mortality in the United States, 1935–2007: Large Racial and Socioeconomic Disparities Have Persisted Over Time. A 75th Anniversary Publication.* Health Resources and Services Administration, Maternal and Child Health Bureau, Rockville, Maryland: U.S. Department of Health and Human Services, 2010.

19. Tamara R. Mose, *The Playdate: Parents, Children, and the New Expectations of Play,* NYU Press, 2016, p. 40.

20. Tim Gill, *No Fear: Growing Up in a Risk Averse Society,* London: Calouste Gulbenkian Foundation, 2007, p. 23.

21. Tamara R. Mose, *The Playdate: Parents, Children, and the New Expectations of Play,* NYU Press, 2016, pp. 10–11.

22. Liana C. Sayer, "Are Parents Investing Less in Children? Trends in Mothers' and Fathers' Time with Children," *American Journal of Sociology,* Vol. 110, No. 1, July 2004, pp. 1–43.

23. Tim Gill, *No Fear: Growing Up in a Risk Averse Society,* London: Calouste Gulbenkian Foundation, 2007, p. 14.

24. Ibid., p. 53.

25. Peter Gray, "The Decline of Play and the Rise of Psychopathology in Children and Adolescents," *American Journal of Play,* Vol. 3, No. 4, Spring 2011, p. 456.

26. U.S. Bureau of the Census, "Table HH-6. Average Population Per Household and Family: 1940 to Present," September 15, 2004.

27. George Gao, "Americans' ideal family size is smaller than it used to be," Pew Research Center, May 8, 2015.

28. Gaia Bernstein and Zvi Triger, "Over-Parenting," *UC Davis Law Review,* Vol. 44, No. 4, 2011, p. 1232.

29. Ibid., p. 1269.

30. Ara Francis, *Family Trouble: Middle-Class Parents, Children's Problems, and the Disruption of Everyday Life,* Rutgers University Press, 2015, p. 113.

31. Linda M. Blum, *Raising Generation Rx: Mothering Kids with Invisible Disabilities in an Age of Inequality,* NYU Press, 2015, p. 239.

32. Ara Francis, *Family Trouble: Middle-Class Parents, Children's Problems, and the Disruption of Everyday Life,* Rutgers University Press, 2015, p. 72.

33. American Psychological Association Zero Tolerance Task Force, "Are Zero Tolerance Policies Effective in the Schools? An Evidentiary Review and Recommendations," *American Psychologist,* Vol. 63, No. 9, December 2008, p. 852.

34. Ibid., pp. 855–856.

35. Mihaly Csikszentmihalyi and Jeremy Hunter, "Happiness in Everyday Life: The Uses of Experience Sampling," *Journal of Happiness Studies,* Vol. 4, No. 2, 2003, pp. 190–196.

36. Mark Ames, Going Postal: *Rage, Murder, and Rebellion: From Reagan's Workplaces to Clinton's Columbine and Beyond,* New York: Soft Skull Press, 2005, p. 197.

Chapter 2: Go to College

1. Sandy Baum and Jennifer Ma, "Trends in College Pricing 2014," The College Board, 2014, p. 17.

2. Heidi Shierholz, Natalie Sabadish, and Nicholas Finio, "Young graduates still face dim job prospects," Economic Policy Institute, April 10, 2013.

3. Ibid.

4. Ben Casselman, "Shut Up About Harvard," *FiveThirtyEight,* March 30, 2016.

5. Sara Goldrick-Rab, *Paying the Price,* University of Chicago Press, 2016, p. 44.

6. Ibid., p. 103.

7. James Dubick, Brandon Mathews, and Clare Cady, "Hunger on Campus: The Challenge of Food Insecurity for College Students," National Student Campaign Against Hunger & Homelessness, October 2016.

8. Department of Education, "Student Loans Overview Fiscal Year 2014 Budget Proposal," p. T-13.

9. Department of Education, "Student Loans Overview Fiscal Year 2014 Budget Proposal," p. 22.

10. The Project on Student Debt at the Institute for College Access & Success, "High Hopes, Big Debts," May 2010.

11. Matthew Reed and Debbie Cochrane, "Student Debt and the Class of 2013," The Project on Student Debt at the Institute for College Access & Success, November 2014.

12. Marc Bousquet, *How the University Works: Higher Education and the Low-Wage Nation,* New York: NYU Press, 2008, p. 2.

13. Donna M. Desrochers and Rita Kirshstein, "Labor Intensive or Labor Expensive? Changing Staffing and Compensation Patterns in Higher Education," The Delta Cost Project at the American Institutes for Research, February 5, 2014, p. 14.

14. Ibid.

15. Marc Bousquet, *How the University Works: Higher Education and the Low-Wage Nation,* New York: NYU Press, 2008, p. 7.

16. Department of Education National Center for Education Statistics, "Digest of Education Statistics, 2012," 2013, Chapter 3.

17. Bob Meister, "They Pledged Your Tuition to Wall Street," *Monthly Review Zine,* November 11, 2009.

18. Sandy Baum and Jennifer Ma, "Trends in College Pricing 2014," The College Board, 2014, p. 17.

19. Eva Bagoty, "U.S. Higher Education Outlook Negative in 2013," Moody's, Report No. 148880, January 16, 2013, p. 5.

20. Ibid., p. 2.

21. Eva Bagoty, "2014 Outlook—US Higher Education, Not-for-Profits and Independent Schools," Moody's, Report No. 160659, November 25, 2013, p. 10.

22. Ibid., p. 2.

23. Donna M. Desrochers and Rita Kirshstein, "Labor Intensive or Labor Expensive? Changing Staffing and Compensation Patterns in Higher Education," The Delta Cost Project at the American Institutes for Research, February 5, 2014, p. 1.

24. Robert C. Dickeson, "Frequently Asked Questions About College Costs," The Secretary of Education's Commission on the Future of Higher Education, 2006, p. 1.

25. Donna M. Desrochers and Rita Kirshstein, "Labor Intensive or Labor Expensive? Changing Staffing and Compensation Patterns in Higher Education," The Delta Cost Project at the American Institutes for Research, February 5, 2014, p. 9.

26. Ibid., p. 7.

27. Office of Senator Elizabeth Warren, "Democratic Senators Highlight Obscene Government Profits Off Student Loan Program," January 31, 2014.

28. United States Government Accountability Office, "Borrower Interest Rates Cannot Be Set in Advance to Precisely and Consistently Balance Federal Revenues and Costs," GAO-14-234, January, 2014.

29. David A. Bergeron and Tobin Van Ostern, "Proposals to Bring Student-Loan Interest Rates Under Control," Center for American Progress, May 23, 2013.

30. Ibid.

31. White House Office of the Press Secretary, "We Can't Wait: Obama Administration to Lower Student Loan Payments for Millions of Borrowers," October 25, 2011.

32. Office of Federal Student Aid at the U.S. Department of Education, "Income-Driven Repayment Plans for Federal Student Loans," July 2014.

33. Congressional Budget Office, "Reestimate of the President's 2014 Mandatory Proposals for Postsecondary Education," 2014.

34. "Uniform Payments Are Smarter if You Have Average Debt," *New York Times,* June 21, 2014.

35. United States Government Accountability Office, "Borrower Interest Rates Cannot Be Set in Advance to Precisely and Consistently Balance Federal Revenues and Costs," GAO-14-234, January, 2014.

36. Department of Education, "Student Loans Overview Fiscal Year 2014 Budget Proposal," p. 4.

37. Ibid., p. 32 (author's calculations).

38. Dylan Matthews, "No, the federal government does not profit off student loans (in some years—see update)," *Washington Post Wonkblog,* May 20, 2013.

39. Department of Education Student Loans Overview Fiscal Year 2014 Budget Proposal, p. 32.

Chapter 3: Work (Sucks)

1. Arne L. Kalleberg, *Good Jobs, Bad Jobs: The Rise of Polarized and Precarious Employment Systems in the United States 1970s to 2000s,* New York: Russell Sage Foundation, 2011, p. 15.

2. Ibid., p. 1.

3. Ibid., p. 10.

4. Ibid., p. 106.

5. Ibid., pp. 110-111.

6. Heidi Shierholz, "Wage Inequality Has Dramatically Increased Among Both Men and Women Over the Last 35 Years," Economic Policy Institute, June 3, 2014.

7. Elise Gould, "Over One-Fourth of Men 25–34 Years Old Earned Poverty-Level Wages in 2013," Economic Policy Institute, June 11, 2014.

8. Elise Gould, "Why America's Workers Need Faster Wage Growth—And What We Can Do About It," Economic Policy Institute, August 27, 2014.

9. Paolo Virno, *A Grammar of the Multitude,* Cambridge, MA: Semiotext(e), 2004, p. 106.

10. David Autor, "The Polarization of Job Opportunities in the U.S. Labor Market Implications for Employment and Earnings," The Hamilton Project at the Center for American Progress, April 2010, p. 4.

11. Ibid., p. 12.

12. Nina Power, *One Dimensional Woman,* Winchester, UK: Zero Books, 2009, p. 18.

13. Hanna Rosin, "The End of Men," *Atlantic,* June 8, 2010.

14. David Autor, "The Polarization of Job Opportunities in the U.S. Labor Market Implications for Employment and Earnings," The Hamilton Project at the Center for American Progress, April 2010, p. 29.

15. Judy Wajcman, *Pressed for Time: The Acceleration of Life in Digital Capitalism,* University of Chicago Press, 2015, p. 68.

16. Jonathan Crary, *24/7: Late Capitalism and the Ends of Sleep,* New York: Verso, 2013, pp. 14–15.

17. Centers for Disease Control and Prevention, "Youth Risk Behavior Surveillance—United States, 2009," MMWR 2010;59, p. 31.

18. National Center for Chronic Disease and Prevention and Health Promotion Division of Adult and Community Health at the Centers for Disease Control and Prevention, "Insufficient Sleep Is a Public Health Epidemic," January 13, 2014.

19. Jonathan Crary, *24/7: Late Capitalism and the Ends of Sleep,* New York: Verso, 2013, p. 41.

20. Lonnie Golden, "Irregular Work Scheduling and Its Consequences," Economic Policy Institute, 2015.

21. Dave Gilson, "Overworked America: 12 Charts That Will Make Your Blood Boil," *Mother Jones,* July/August 2011.

22. Arne L. Kalleberg, *Good Jobs, Bad Jobs,* New York: Russell Sage Foundation, 2011, pp. 155–156.

23. Bureau of Labor Statistics, "Median Duration of Unemployment," retrieved from FRED, Federal Reserve Bank of St. Louis, November 21, 2014.

24. Bureau of Labor Statistics, "Employment Level—Part-Time for Economic Reasons, All Industries," retrieved from FRED, Federal Reserve Bank of St. Louis, November 21, 2014.

25. Lawrence Mishel, "Declining value of the federal minimum wage is a major factor driving inequality," Economic Policy Institute, February 21, 2013.

26. Bureau of Labor Statistics, "Union Members—2013," USDL-14-0095, January 24, 2014.

27. Ibid.

28. Ibid.

29. Bureau of Labor Statistics, "Major Work Stoppages in 2013," USDL-14-0217, February 12, 2014, pp. 3–4.

30. Bureau of Labor Statistics, "Union Members—2013," USDL-14-0095, January 24, 2014.

31. Ibid.

32. Phil Gardner, "The Debate Over Unpaid College Internships," Intern Bridge Inc., 2011.

33. Ross Perlin, *Intern Nation,* New York: Verso, 2011, p. 27.

34. National Association of Colleges and Employers, "2013 Student Survey," 2013. *Note: The NACE has since suppressed the report, but with a little help from the Internet Archive's Wayback Machine readers can find it.*

35. Phil Gardner, "The Debate Over Unpaid College Internships," Intern Bridge Inc., 2011.

36. Phil Gardner, "The Debate Over Unpaid College Internships," Intern Bridge Inc., 2011.

37. Joseph E. Aoun et al., letter to the Department of Labor, April 28, 2010.

38. Ross Perlin, *Intern Nation,* New York: Verso, 2011, p. 126.

39. Caroline Ratcliffe and Signe-Mary McKernan, "Lost Generations? Wealth Building Among the Young," Urban Institute, March 19, 2013.

40. Ibid.

41. Raj Chetty, David Grusky, Maximilian Hell, Nathaniel Hendren, Robert Manduca, and Jimmy Narang, "The Fading American Dream: Trends in Absolute Income Mobility Since 1940," NBER Working Paper No. 22910, December 2016.

42. Yuliya Demyanyk and Matthew Koepke, "Americans Cut Their Debt," Federal Reserve Bank of Cleveland, August 8, 2012.

43. Richard Fry, "Young Adults, Student Debt and Economic Well-Being," Pew Research and Social and Demographic Trends, May 14, 2014.

44. Neil Shah, "U.S. Household Net Worth Hits Record High," *Wall Street Journal,* March 6, 2014.

45. Board of Governors of the Federal Reserve System, "Financial Accounts of the United States Flow of Funds, Balance Sheets, and Integrated Macroeconomic Accounts Second Quarter 2014," September 18, 2014, p. 16.

46. Ibid., p. 13.

47. Ibid., p. 138.

48. Ibid., p. 13. Compensation and profits are reported on different schedules; I've used the most up-to-date material where I can. Please forgive the slightly disjointed time periods.

49. Pew Research Center, "On Pay Gap, Millennial Women Near Parity—For Now," December 11, 2013, p. 10.

50. Kevin Roose, *Young Money: Inside the Hidden World of Wall Street's Post-Crash Recruits,* New York: Grand Central Publishing, 2014, p. 20.

51. Ibid., p. 35.

52. Ibid., p. 114.

53. John Schmitt, "The Minimum Wage Is Too Damn Low," Center for Economic and Policy Research, March 2012.

54. Kevin Roose, *Young Money,* New York: Grand Central Publishing, 2014, p. 35.

55. Ibid., p. 283.

Chapter 4: The Feds

1. Mara Liasson, "Conservative Advocate," *National Public Radio,* May 25, 2001.

2. The Congressional Budget Office, "The Budget and Economic Outlook: 2014 to 2024," February 2014, p. 156.

3. Adam Looney and Michael Greenstone, "A Record Decline in Government Jobs: Implications for the Economy and America's Workforce," The Hamilton Project at the Center for American Progress, August 2012.

4. "Annual Review of Government Contracting," National Contract Management Association and Bloomberg Business, pp. 4–5.

5. "Contractors: How Much Are They Costing the Government?," Senate Hearing 112-615, U.S. Government Printing Office, March 29, 2012, p. 51.

6. "Fed Figures 2013—Hiring at a Glance," Partnership for Public Service, September 10, 2013.

7. Nate Silver, "Health Care Drives Increase in Government Spending," *New York Times,* January 17, 2013.

8. Ibid.

9. Centers for Medicare and Medicaid Services, "NHE summary including share of GDP, CY 1960–2012," Table 1.

10. Gary V. Engelhardt and Jonathan Gruber, "Social Security and the Evolution of Elderly Poverty," National Bureau of Economic Research Working Paper No. 10466, May 2004.

11. Social Security Administration, "The 2014 Annual Report of the Board of Trustees of the Federal Old-Age and Survivors Insurance and Federal Disability Insurance Trust Funds," July 28, 2014, p. 4.

12. Ibid.

13. C. Eugene Steuerle and Caleb Quakenbush, "Social Security and Medicare Taxes and Benefits over a Lifetime," Urban Institute, November 2013.

14. Pew Research Center, "Millennials in Adulthood," March 7, 2014, p. 37.

15. C. Eugene Steuerle and Caleb Quakenbush, "Social Security and Medicare Taxes and Benefits over a Lifetime," Urban Institute, November 2013.

16. American Association of Retired Persons, "AARP Annual Report 2013," p. 51.

17. American Association of Retired Persons, "AARP Services, Inc. Annual Report 2013," p. 39.

18. Open Secrets at the Center for Responsive Politics, "Influence and Lobbying Summary: AARP," 2013.

19. Stanford Center for Poverty and Inequality, "The Poverty and Inequality Report 2014," January 13, 2014, p. 14.

20. Center on Budget and Policy Priorities, "Chart Book: TANF at 18," August 22, 2014.

21. Department of Health and Human Services, "Administration for Children and Families Justification of Estimates for Appropriations Committees—Temporary Assistance for Needy Families," p. 282.

22. Center on Budget and Policy Priorities, "Chart Book: TANF at 20," August 5, 2016.

23. Stanford Center for Poverty and Inequality, "The Poverty and Inequality Report 2014," January 13, 2014, p. 14.

24. Ibid.

25. "No Child Left Behind Act of 2001," Public Law 107–110, January 8, 2002, 115 STAT. 1448–1449.

26. Ibid., 1466.

27. Ibid., 1479.

28. Bob Schaeffer, "50+ Ways Schools 'Cheat' on Testing: Manipulating High-Stakes Exam Scores for Political Gain," FairTest: National Center for Fair & Open Testing, July 7, 2014.

29. Nicole Nguyen, *A Curriculum of Fear,* Minneapolis: University of Minnesota Press, p. 141.

30. Ibid., p. 165.

31. Ibid., p. 118.

32. "American Recovery and Reinvestment Act of 2009," Public Law 111-5 Notice of Final Priorities Appendix B, November 18, 2009, p. 2.

33. Ibid.

34. Ibid.

35. Common Core State Standards Initiative, "Frequently Asked Questions," p. 1.

36. Daniel J. Losen and Tia Elena Martinez, "Out of School & Off Track: The Overuse of Suspensions in American Middle and High Schools," Center for Civil Rights Remedies at the UCLA Civil Rights Project, April 8, 2013.

37. Daniel J. Losen and Russell J. Skiba, "Suspended Education Urban Middle Schools in Crisis," Southern Poverty Law Center, September 13, 2010, p. 10.

38. Department of Justice Bureau of Justice Statistics, "National Crime Victimization Survey (NCVS), 1992–2011," Table S2.1.

39. Daniel J. Losen and Russell J. Skiba, "Suspended Education Urban Middle Schools in Crisis," Southern Poverty Law Center, September 13, 2010, p. 3.

40. Daniel J. Losen and Tia Elena Martinez, "Out of School & Off Track: The Overuse of Suspensions in American Middle and High Schools," Center for Civil Rights Remedies at the UCLA Civil Rights Project, April 8, 2013, p. 1.

41. Department of Education Office for Civil Rights, "Civil Rights Data Collection: Data Snapshot (School Discipline)," March 21, 2014, p. 7.

42. Kathleen Nolan, *Police in the Hallways: Discipline in an Urban High School,* Minneapolis: University of Minnesota Press, 2011, p. 40.

43. Ibid., p. 111.

44. Jonathan Chait, "Barack Obama, Ta-Nehisi Coates, Poverty, and Culture," *New York,* March 19, 2014.

45. Victor M. Rios, *Punished: Policing the Lives of Black and Latino Boys,* New York: NYU Press, 2011, p. 21.

46. Ibid., p. 81.

47. Ibid., p. 29.

48. Robert Brame, Michael G. Turner, Raymond Paternoster, and Shawn D. Bushway, "Cumulative Prevalence of Arrest from Ages 8 to 23 in a National Sample," *Pediatrics,* Vol. 129, No. 1, January 2012, p. 23.

49. Pamela E. Oliver and Marino A. Bruce, "Tracking the Causes and Consequences of Racial Disparities in Imprisonment," Proposal to the National Science Foundation, August 2001, p. 3.

50. Michelle Alexander, *The New Jim Crow: Mass Incarceration in the Age of Colorblindness,* New York: New Press, 2010, p. 9.

Chapter 5: Everybody Is a Star

1. Mike Sager, "Todd Marinovich: The Man Who Never Was," *Esquire,* May 2009.
2. Douglas S. Looney, "Bred to Be a Superstar," *Sports Illustrated,* February 1988.
3. Anthony R. Anzell, Jeffrey A. Potteiger, William J. Kraemer, and Sango Otieno, "Changes in Height, Body Weight, and Body Composition in American Football Players From 1942 to 2011," *Journal of Strength and Conditioning Research,* Vol. 27, No. 2, February 2013, p. 277.
4. Viraj Sanghvi, "How has height changed over time in the NBA?," *To the Mean,* August 26, 2014.
5. Dan Diamond, "NBA Draft: Is Being 7 Feet Tall the Fastest Way to Get Rich in America?," *Forbes,* June 27, 2013.
6. Bernard Malamud, *The Natural,* New York: Farrar, Straus, and Giroux, 1952 (2003), p. 10.
7. Major League Baseball, "2014 Opening Day Rosters Feature 224 Players Born Outside the U.S.," April 1, 2014.
8. Bruce Kelley and Carl Carchia, " 'Hey, data data—swing!' The hidden demographics of youth sports," *ESPN The Magazine,* July 11, 2013.
9. Ibid.
10. Rachel Bachman, "ESPN Strikes Deal for College Football Playoff," *Wall Street Journal,* November 21, 2012.
11. Chris Smith, "The Most Valuable Conferences in College Sports 2014," *Forbes,* April 15, 2014.
12. Brian Burnsed, "Athletics departments that make more than they spend still a minority," NCAA.org, September 18, 2015.
13. American Gaming Association, "Fact Sheets—Sports Wagering," 2014.
14. Taylor Branch, "The Shame of College Sports," *Atlantic,* September 7, 2011.
15. NCAA Research, "Division I Results from the NCAA GOALS Study on the Student-Athlete Experience," FARA Annual Meeting and Symposium, November 2011, p. 17.
16. Ramogi Huma and Ellen J. Staurowsky, "The $6 Billion Heist: Robbing College Athletes Under the Guise of Amateurism," NCPA and Drexel University Department of Sport Management, 2012, p. 13.
17. Ibid., p. 3.
18. Ibid., p. 13.
19. *Edward O'Bannon et al. v. National Collegiate Athletic Association, Electronic Arts Inc. and Collegiate Licensing Co.,* U.S. District Court Northern District of California, C 09-3329 CW, August 8, 2014, p. 41.

20. Ibid., p. 56.
21. Ibid.
22. Darren Heitner, "March Madness Makes Millions For Burgeoning Collegiate Licensing Business," *Forbes,* April 3, 2015.
23. National Football Foundation, "Colleges and Universities Continue Adding Football Teams in 2014," July 16, 2014.
24. Brian Burnsed, "Participation rates continue to rise," NCAA News, October 18, 2013.
25. NCAA Research, "Probability of competing beyond high school," September 2013.
26. Ibid.
27. Taylor Swift, "For Taylor Swift, the Future of Music Is a Love Story," *Wall Street Journal,* July 7, 2014.
28. Izabela Wagner, *Producing Excellence: The Making of Virtuosos,* Rutgers University Press, 2015, p. 191.
29. Ibid., p. 45.
30. Natalie Coulter, *Tweening the Girl: The Crystallization of the Tween Market,* New York: Peter Lang Publishing, 2014.
31. "'Hannah Montana' Finale Sets Disney Ratings Record," *Billboard,* January 19, 2011.
32. Sarah Oliver, *She Can't Stop: Miley Cyrus: The Biography,* London: John Blake Publishers, 2014, p. 12.
33. Keith Caulfield, "Ariana Grande Debuts at No. 1 on Billboard 200," *Billboard,* September 11, 2013.
34. Susanne Ault, "Survey: YouTube Stars More Popular Than Mainstream Celebs Among U.S. Teens," *Variety,* August 5, 2014.
35. Shama Hyder, "7 Things You Can Do to Build an Awesome Personal Brand," *Forbes,* August 18, 2014.
36. Taylor Swift, "For Taylor Swift, the Future of Music Is a Love Story," *Wall Street Journal,* July 7, 2014.
37. Alex Pappademas, "Lex Luger Can Write a Hit Rap Song in the Time It Takes to Read This," *New York Times Magazine,* November 6, 2011.
38. Alexander Iadarola, "13 Things All Fruity Loops Producers Know to Be True," *Fader,* October 31, 2014.
39. Michael Humphrey, "Datpiff: How Love for Mixtapes Grew to Lil Wayne Levels," *Forbes,* August 4, 2011.

Chapter 6: Behavior Modification

1. Pew Research Center Social and Demographic Trends, "Millennials in Adulthood," March 7, 2014, p. 7.

2. Jean M. Twenge, "The Age of Anxiety? Birth Cohort Change in Anxiety and Neuroticism, 1952–1993," *Journal of Personality and Social Psychology,* Vol. 79, No. 6, 2000, p. 1007.

3. Ibid., p. 1017.

4. Jean M. Twenge, Brittany Gentile, C. Nathan DeWall, Debbie Ma, Katharine Lacefield, and David R. Schurtz, "Birth cohort increases in psychopathology among young Americans, 1938–2007: A cross-temporal meta-analysis of the MMPI," *Clinical Psychology Review,* 2010, p. 153.

5. Mark Olfson, Marc J. Gameroff, Steven C. Marcus, and Peter S. Jensen, "National Trends in the Treatment of Attention Deficit Hyperactivity Disorder," *American Journal of Psychiatry,* Vol. 160, No. 6, June 2003.

6. Susanna N. Visser et al., "Trends in the Parent-Report of Health Care Provider-Diagnosed and Medicated Attention-Deficit/Hyperactivity Disorder: United States, 2003–2011," *Journal of the American Academy of Child & Adolescent Psychiatry,* Vol. 53, No. 1, January 2014, p. 37.

7. Tanya E. Froehlich, "Prevalence, Recognition, and Treatment of Attention-Deficit/Hyperactivity Disorder in a National Sample of US Children," *Archives of Pediatrics & Adolescent Medicine,* Vol. 161, No. 9, September 2007, p. 863.

8. U.S. Department of Education, "Children with ADD/ADHD—Topic Brief," March 1999.

9. Sean Esteban McCabe, John R. Knight, Christian J. Teter, and Henry Wechsler, "Nonmedical use of prescription stimulants among US college students: prevalence and correlates from a national survey," *Addiction,* Vol. 100, No. 1, January 2005, p. 99.

10. Susanna N. Visser et al., "Trends in the Parent-Report of Health Care Provider-Diagnosed and Medicated Attention-Deficit/Hyperactivity Disorder: United States, 2003–2011," *Journal of the American Academy of Child & Adolescent Psychiatry,* Vol. 53, No. 1, January 2014, p. 34.

11. Jean M. Twenge and Stacy M. Campbell, "Generational differences in psychological traits and their impact on the workplace," *Journal of Managerial Psychology,* Vol. 23, No. 8, 2008, pp. 870–871.

12. Catherine Rampell, "The Half-Trillion-Dollar Depression," *New York Times,* July 7, 2013.

13. Julie Magno Zito et al., "Trends in the Prescribing of Psychotropic Medications to Preschoolers," *JAMA,* Vol. 283, No. 8, February 2000, p. 1027.

14. Cindy Parks Thomas, Peter Conrad, Rosemary Casler, and Elizabeth Goodman, "Trends in the Use of Psychotropic Medications Among Adolescents, 1994 to 2001," *Psychiatric Services,* Vol. 57, No. 1, January 2006.

15. Ibid.

16. Mark Olfson and Steven C. Marcus, "National Patterns in Antidepressant Medication Treatment," *JAMA Psychiatry,* Vol. 66, No. 8, August 2009.

17. Jeremy A. Greene and David Herzberg, "Hidden in Plain Sight: Marketing Prescription Drugs to Consumers in the Twentieth Century," *American Journal of Public Health,* Vol. 100, No. 5, May 2010, p. 793.

18. C. Lee Ventola, "Direct-to-Consumer Pharmaceutical Advertising: Therapeutic or Toxic?," *Pharmacy and Therapeutics,* Vol. 36, No. 10, October 2011, p. 670.

19. Ibid., p. 669.

20. Matthew K. Nock et al., "Suicide and Suicidal Behavior," *Epidemiology Review,* Vol. 30, No. 1, October 2008, p. 26.

21. Alice Robb, "Twitter Is for Narcissists, Facebook Is for Egotists," *New Republic,* January 15, 2014.

22. Tracy Packiam Alloway, "Selfies, Facebook, and Narcissism: What's the Link?," *Psychology Today,* May 11, 2014.

23. Stephen Marche, "Is Facebook Making Us Lonely?," *Atlantic,* May 2012.

24. Taylor Lorenz, "Inside the secret meeting that changed the fate of Vine forever," Mic.com, October 29, 2016.

25. Pew Research Center Internet Project Survey, "Internet User Demographics," January 2017.

26. Mary Madden, "Teens and Technology 2013," Pew Research Center's Internet & American Life Project, March 13, 2013, p. 4.

27. Department of Education National Center for Education Statistics, "The Condition of Education 2006," (NCES 2007–064), 2006, Indicator 19.

28. Rob Horning, "'Sharing' Economy and Self-Exploitation," Remarks at *Rhizome*'s Internet Subjects: #Uberwar and the "Sharing" Economy, June 11, 2014.

29. S. Parker Yesko, "Facebook-funded police substation to open in Menlo Park," *San Francisco Examiner,* April 25, 2014.

30. danah boyd, *It's Complicated: The Social Lives of Networked Teens,* New Haven: Yale University Press, 2014, pp. 21–22.

31. Ibid.

32. Anne Hoffman, "Petitioner Fights 'Pay to Play' in Mission Soccer," *MissionLocal,* October 1, 2012.

33. MissionCreekVideo, "Mission Playground Is Not for Sale," YouTube, September 25, 2014.

34. Katherine Losse, *The Boy Kings: A Journey into the Heart of the Social Network,* New York: Free Press, 2012, p. 54.

35. Ibid., p. 193.

36. Ibid., p. 141.

37. John Palfrey and Urs Gasser, *Born Digital: How Children Grow Up in a Digital Age (Revised and Expanded)*, New York: Basic Books, 2016, p. 123.

38. Jodi Dean, *Blog Theory: Feedback and Capture in the Circuits of Drive*, Cambridge, UK: Polity Press, 2010, pp. 3–4.

39. Ibid.

40. Aaron Smith, "African Americans and Technology Use," Pew Research Center, January 6, 2014, p. 10.

41. danah boyd, *It's Complicated: The Social Lives of Networked Teens*, New Haven: Yale University Press, 2014, p. 74.

42. Ibid., p. 64.

43. Lloyd D. Johnston et al., "2013 Overview Key Findings on Adolescent Drug Use," University of Michigan Institute for Social Research, February 2014, pp. 11–12.

44. Art Swift, "For First Time, Americans Favor Legalizing Marijuana," *Gallup*, October 22, 2013.

45. Andrew Leonard, "How LSD Microdosing Became the Hot New Business Trip," *Rolling Stone*, November 20, 2015.

46. Lloyd D. Johnston et al., "2013 Overview Key Findings on Adolescent Drug Use," University of Michigan Institute for Social Research, February 2014, pp. 9–10.

47. Susan T. Ennet, Nancy S. Tobler, Christopher L. Ringwalt, and Robert L. Flewelling, "How Effective Is Drug Abuse Resistance Education? A Meta-Analysis of Project DARE Outcome Evaluations," *American Journal of Public Health*, September 1994, Vol. 84, No. 9.

48. Centers for Disease Control, "Today's Heroin Epidemic Infographics," July 2015.

49. Zusha Elinson, "Aging Baby Boomers Bring Drug Habits into Middle Age," *Wall Street Journal*, March 16, 2015.

50. Ibid.

51. Lawrence B. Finer and Jesse M. Philbin, "Sexual Initiation, Contraceptive Use, and Pregnancy Among Young Adolescents," *Pediatrics*, Vol. 131, No. 5, May 2013, p. 889.

52. Centers for Disease Control and Prevention, "Trends in the Prevalence of Sexual Behaviors and HIV Testing National YRBS: 1991–2013," June 2014.

53. Guttmacher Institute, "Fact Sheet—American Teens' Sexual and Reproductive Health," May 2014.

54. Kathryn Kost and Stanley Henshaw, "U.S. Teenage Pregnancies, Births and Abortions, 2010: National and State Trends by Age, Race and Ethnicity," Guttmacher Institute, May 2014.

55. Pew Research Center's Forum on Religion & Public Life, "Religion Among the Millennials," February 2010, p. 1.

56. David Finkelhor and Lisa Jones, "Why Have Child Maltreatment and Child Victimization Declined?," *Journal of Social Issues*, Vol. 62, No. 4, 2006, pp. 686–687.

57. Department of Health and Human Services Children's Bureau, "Child Maltreatment 2012," December 17, 2013, p. 92.

58. David Finkelhor and Lisa Jones, "Why Have Child Maltreatment and Child Victimization Declined?," *Journal of Social Issues,* Vol. 62, No. 4, 2006, p. 686.

59. Centers for Disease Control and Prevention, "Trends in the Prevalence of Sexual Behaviors and HIV Testing National YRBS: 1991–2013," June 2014.

60. Lawrence B. Finer and Jesse M. Philbin, "Sexual Initiation, Contraceptive Use, and Pregnancy Among Young Adolescents," *Pediatrics,* Vol. 131, No. 5, May 2013, Table 2.

61. Jeff R. Temple et al., "Teen Sexting and Its Association with Sexual Behaviors," *Archives of Pediatrics & Adolescent Medicine,* Vol. 166, No. 9, September 2012, p. 828.

62. Jeff R. Temple and HyeJeong Choi, "Longitudinal Association Between Teen Sexting and Sexual Behavior," *Pediatrics,* Vol. 134, No. 5, November 2014, p. 4.

63. John Palfrey and Urs Gasser, *Born Digital: How Children Grow Up in a Digital Age (Revised and Expanded),* New York, NY: Basic Books, p. 91.

64. Model Alliance, "Industry Analysis," accessed November 24, 2014.

65. Pornhub Insights, "What Women Want," September 16, 2014.

66. Michele L. Ybarra and Kimberly J. Mitchell, "Exposure to Internet Pornography among Children and Adolescents: A National Survey," *Cyberpsychology & Behavior* Vol. 8, No. 5, 2005. (To be fair, these are Canadian teens, but given the subject matter, I'd sooner look at Canadian teens than a comparable but older American study, and this is the most recent.)

67. Lucia F. O'Sullivan (2014), "Linking online sexual activities to health outcomes among teens." In E. S. Lefkowitz & S. A. Vasilenko (Eds.), *Positive and negative outcomes of sexual behaviors. New Directions for Child and Adolescent Development* No. 144, pp. 37–51.

68. Katrina Forrester, "Making Sense of Modern Pornography," *New Yorker,* September 26, 2016.

69. David Auerbach, "Vampire Porn," *Slate,* October 23, 2014.

Conclusion

1. U.S. EPA, "Future of Climate Change," accessed January 1, 2017.

2. Julia Angwin and Terry Parris Jr., "Facebook Lets Advertisers Exclude Users by Race," *ProPublica,* October 28, 2016.

3. Shane Snow, "How Soylent and Oculus Could Fix the Prison System (A Thought Experiment)," maneatingrobot.

4. David Cotter and Joan Hermsen, "Back on Track? The Stall and Rebound in Support for Women's New Roles in Work and Politics, 1977–2012," Council on Contemporary Families, July 2014.

5. Donna Lee King, *Doing Their Share to Save the Planet: Children and Environmental Crisis,* New Brunswick: Rutgers University Press, 1995, p. 27.

6. "Beyond Distrust: How Americans View Their Government," Pew Research Center, 2015.

7. "2016 Presidential Race," Opensecrets.org.

8. Richard Fry, "Millennials Match Boomers as Largest Generation in U.S. Electorate, But Will They Vote?" Pew Research Center, May 16, 2016.

9. Connie Cass, "Young Generation No Slouch at Volunteering," Associated Press, December 29, 2014.

10. Philanthropy Roundtable, "Output of Nonprofit Sector," Statistics Almanac, 2016.

11. Mike Konczal, "Parsing the Data and Ideology of the We Are 99% Tumblr," Rortybomb, October 9, 2011.

Graph Credits

Index